Three Philosophies
and
One Reality

&

NHK Radio Talks

by
Gudo Wafu Nishijima

DOGEN SANGHA PUBLICATIONS

Dogen Sangha Publications

www.dogensangha.org

First edition 2009

© 2009 Gudo Nishijima

ISBN   978-0-9562999-2-5

Part I of this book is based on a booklet entitled "Three Philosophies and One Reality" that was edited and produced by Michael Luetchford. Part II is based on a translation of three talks which Master Gudo Nishijima gave on NHK Radio 1 in Japan in December 1994. The talks were translated and edited by Yoko & Michael Luetchford and were originally published as a booklet entitled "Buddhism & Action". This paperback version was edited and produced by Peter Rocca.

Cover photo by Jürgen Seggelke.

Gudo Nishijima was born in Yokohama, Japan in November 1919, and graduated from the Law Department of Tokyo University in September 1946. In October 1940 he first met Master Kodo Sawaki, whose teaching he received until Master Kodo's death in December 1965. During this time, he combined the daily practice of Zazen and study of Shobogenzo with a career at the Japanese Ministry of Finance and at a securities financing company. In December 1973 he became a priest under the late Master Renpo Niwa, and in December 1977 he received the transmission of Dharma from the same Master (who subsequently became the abbot of Eihei-ji temple). Shortly thereafter he became a consultant to the Ida Ryogokudo company, and in 1987 established the Ida Ryogokudo Zazen Dojo in Ichikawa City near Tokyo. He gave instruction in Zazen, and lectures on Master Dogen's works, in Japanese and in English, for many years in Tokyo and Osaka and at Tokei-in temple in Shizuoka prefecture. Gudo Nishijima's other publications in English include a translation of Master Dogen's "Shobogenzo" (with co-translator Chodo Cross) in four volumes, "To Meet the Real Dragon" (with Jeffrey Bailey), and a translation of Mater Dogen's collection of 301 Zen stories (koans) "Shinji Shobogenzo". He has published a Japanese translation of Master Nagarjuna's Mulamadhyamakakarika, and is presently at work on an English translation. He also writes a blog about Buddhism and current affairs.

Three Philosophies
and
One Reality

&

NHK Radio Talks

TABLE OF CONTENTS

INTRODUCTION

The first part of this book is an edited collection of seven talks on Buddhism which I gave to a weekly seminar I held in Tokyo for many years. The second part is a translation of three talks I gave on NHK Radio 1 in Japan in December 1994.

In the first part, I discuss my interpretation of Gautama Buddha's Four Noble Truths. I call my theory the *Three Philosophies and One Reality*. I base this theory on my understanding of the *Shobogenzo*, a book that was written in the thirteenth century by a Japanese Buddhist priest and philosopher known as Master Dogen. I have read and studied the *Shobogenzo* since I first became interested in Buddhism as a teenager. After reading the *Shobogenzo* over and over many times, I noticed that Master Dogen wrote the *Shobogenzo* in a very special way; using a unique pattern of expression.

The ideas in the *Shobogenzo* are based on a pattern of four phases. First, Master Dogen explains a problem from the idealistic point of view; that is, using abstract concepts. Then he explains the same problem, but this time from the objective, or material point of view, with concrete examples and facts. Then he explains the problem a third time as a real problem; that is, realistically thinking. And finally, he tries to suggest the nature of reality itself.

The *Shobogenzo* is full of these four-phased explanations. So when we read the *Shobogenzo*, Master Dogen often appears to contradict what he has said in a previous sentence. However, after I had read and re-read Master Dogen's book, I realized Master Dogen was attempting to discuss all problems from three points of view, subjective and theoretical, objective and material, and realistic. He then insists on the difference between his three viewpoints and the real situation itself.

I believe that Master Dogen's way of explaining Buddhism using a pattern of four phases is related to Gautama Buddha's Four Noble Truths, which were the subject of his first sermon to his former companions after his enlightenment. Based on my understanding of Master Dogen's four ways of explaining Buddhism, I developed my theory of *Three Philosophies and One Reality*. And based on my belief in Master Dogen's Buddhist ideas, I believe that the *Three Philosophies and One Reality* may be the true interpretation of the Four Noble Truths.

But although theories are important in Buddhism, Buddhism teaches us to never lose sight of the real situation in our everyday life itself. Buddhism says that the most important matter for each of us is how we act in the real world. In the NHK Radio Talks in the second part of this book, I discuss Buddhism from the viewpoint of our action in everyday life.

I would like to express my thanks to everyone who came to my lectures and zazen practice in Tokyo and other locations over many years. Without the many questions and discussions at those lectures, this book would not have been possible in its present form.

Gudo Wafu Nishijima

Tokyo

2009

PART I

Three Philosophies

&

One Reality

Edited by
Michael Luetchford

CHAPTER ONE
THE THEORY OF FOUR VIEWS
_____ ᬏᬓᬒ _____

The Central Theory of Buddhism

Buddhist theory is a vast philosophical system. For this reason it is impossible to give a complete overview of the many theories in only a single lecture. However, I would like to start by explaining the most important of these theories, and one which is central to all Buddhist thought. This is the *Theory of Four Views;* my interpretation of the Sanskrit words *catvary aryasatyani*. This phrase is usually translated as the *Four Noble Truths*.

The Four Noble Truths

Buddhist Scriptures tell us that after Gautama Buddha attained the truth, he wanted to teach others what he had learned. But he also had some doubt as to whether people would be able to understand his theory, because of its complexity. Tradition says that a god from heaven gave him great encouragement to give his first sermon, and so he went ahead. His first sermon was preached to his five former companions with whom he studied asceticism. We are told that in this first sermon he preached the *Four Noble Truths*, or in my translation, the *Theory of Four Views*, and the *Middle Way*. This is

1

why we think of these two teachings as the central theories of Buddhism. To understand these theories is to understand the core of the Buddhist philosophical system. Unfortunately, many people studying Buddhism in the present age have not had the chance to do so yet, especially in western countries.

The Traditional Interpretation

Traditionally, *catvary aryasatyani*, or the *Four Noble Truths* are:

Duhkha-satya -	The Truth of Suffering
Samudaya-satya -	The Truth of Aggregates (The Origin of Suffering)
Nirodha-satya -	The Truth of Cessation or Denial (The Destruction of Suffering)
Marga-satya -	The Truth of the Right Way

When I was a teenager, I read about the *Four Noble Truths* in Buddhist books, but I could not understand what they were referring to at all. So these four truths, which were said to be the core of Buddhism itself, became a hindrance, or stumbling block in my efforts to study Buddhism. If we look in old scriptures, the Theravada Buddhist Scriptures for example, we can find traditional explanations of the meaning of these *Four Noble Truths*. They explain that the *Truth of Suffering* means that all things and events in this world are suffering; that the *Truth of Aggregates* means that all suffering derives from human desire; that the *Truth of Cessation or Denial* means that we must destroy our desire; and the *Truth of the Right Way* means that, having destroyed our desire, we can find the right way.

But I can find no real meaning in these explanations, no

matter how hard I try. If all things and events in this world are suffering, then Buddhism can be at best a dogmatic and pessimistic religion. If all suffering results from human desire, then Buddhism can be no more than asceticism. If the idea of destroying all our desires was a Buddhist idea, than Buddhism must be a religion which advocates what is impossible; for it is utterly impossible for us to destroy our desires. Desire is the basis of our human existence itself.

The *Truth of the Right Way* is further explained as the *Eightfold Noble Path*; right view, right thinking, right speech, right behavior, right livelihood, right effort, right state of body, and right state of mind. But I cannot find any relationship between this fourth truth and the first three.

The *Shobogenzo* and The Four Views

When I was eighteen, I found a book called the *Shobogenzo*. It was written in the thirteenth century by the founder of the sect of Buddhism in Japan which is based on the practice of Zazen. His name is Master Dogen. I found the *Shobogenzo* almost impossible to read at that time, and I was amazed that there could be a book written in Japanese which I was unable to understand at all. But although I could not understand it, I had the feeling that the book might contain important and valuable things. This was the start of what was to become forty years of study. And when at last I could understand the meaning of the *Shobogenzo*, it also became clear to me why I had found it so difficult for so long. The book itself is composed of many contradictory statements, and this made it appear illogical. But after reading and re-reading it many times, I found that the *Shobogenzo* is in fact constructed in a very special way; using a unique pattern of expression.

Master Dogen expresses his ideas in the *Shobogenzo* based on a pattern of four phases. First, he explains a problem from the idealistic point of view; that is, as an idea using abstract concepts. Then, immediately after this first phase, he explains the same problem, but this time from the objective, or material point of view. In other words, he gives concrete examples and facts. Then, in the next phase, he explains the problem yet a third time as a real problem; that is, realistically thinking. Of course, it is very difficult for him to explain the reality surrounding the problem with words in a book, but he attempts to do so by bringing together the subjective viewpoint which he presents first, and the second objective viewpoint. He synthesizes the two viewpoints into a realistic appraisal of the problem; a synthesis of the self and the external world. And in the final phase, he tries to suggest the subtle ineffable nature of reality itself by using symbolic, poetic, or figurative forms of speech.

The *Shobogenzo* is full of these four-phased explanations. The chapters themselves fall into four groups: theoretical, objective, realistic, and symbolic, figurative or poetic. The contents of the chapters are also divided in the same way, and even the content of individual paragraphs follows the same pattern. In general, a theoretical or subjective explanation and a materialistic or objective explanation of the same problem will always be contradictory. Again, a realistic explanation will seemingly be in contradiction to both the subjective and objective points of view. And the real situation itself is different again from the realistic explanation given. So when we first read the *Shobogenzo*, we are astounded by what appear to be gross contradictions in logic. This is one of the reasons why the book is difficult to understand. It appears full of opposing ideas.

However, after I had read and re-read Master Dogen's book, I got used to this unique way of thinking about things. He discusses all problems from three points of view, subjective and theoretical, objective and material, and realistic. He then insists on the difference between his three viewpoints and the real situation itself. Using this method, he is able to explain the reality of a situation very clearly and logically. He believes that the most important thing is to see what the reality itself is; and at the same time, he realizes how impossible this is using the medium of the written word.

So this unique pattern or logical system is Master Dogen's way of suggesting what reality is. And I believe that Master Dogen's method is in fact a very realistic way of explaining reality. I found that Master Dogen's ideas were very realistic, and I found too that Buddhism is a religion of reality.

Then I remembered the *Four Noble Truths* which had defeated me so completely. I could not help seeing a link between the four-phased pattern in Master Dogen's works and the *Four Noble Truths*. Then I started to think that possibly the biggest contradiction which Gautama Buddha must have faced in his thinking would have been between the subjective, idealistic thought of traditional Indian religion and the objective, materialist philosophies of the six great philosophers who were popular in India at that time.

I thought that Gautama Buddha's solution to this contradiction was his discovery that we are in fact living in reality; not, as idealists tend to think, in the world of ideas, or as materialists tend to think, in a world of objective matter alone. Gautama Buddha established his own philosophy based on the fact that we live in the world of momentary existence, in the real world itself. But to express this real world in words is impossible. So he used a method which brought together the two fundamental philosophical viewpoints into a synthesized whole. And the philosophical system he constructed in this way is the Buddhist philosophical system. But at the same time, he realized that philosophy is not reality; it is only discussion of the nature of reality. He needed some method with which people could see directly what the nature of reality is. This method is Zazen, a practice which was already traditional in India from ancient times. Gautama Buddha found that when we sit in this traditional posture in quietness, we can see directly what reality is. So he recommended his disciples to practice Zazen every day.

This is the way in which I found my new interpretation of the *Four Noble Truths*. I thought that *duhkha-satya*, or the *Truth of Suffering*, was the ancient Indian way of expressing idealistic philosophy. When we are full of ideals and anxious to realize those ideals, we invariably suffer from being unable to realize them.

I thought that *samudaya-satya* or the *Truth of Aggregates* might in fact refer to aggregates of *paramanu*, the Sanskrit word for the smallest particle of matter in existence - the modern atom. The *Truth of Aggregates* would thus refer to a primitive science of matter, to the philosophy of materialism as it existed at that time.

Then I interpreted *nirodha-satya*, the *Truth of Cessation or Denial*, to mean a dialectic synthesis; a negation of idealism and materialism.

In the ultimate stage, philosophies can never be reality itself. Gautama Buddha found this fact. And so *marga-satya*, the *Truth of the Right Way* is his recommendation to practice Zazen.

So my new interpretation gave four truths: idealism, materialism, realism and reality itself. This fundamental four-fold structure is of great importance in understanding Buddhist theory. Gautama Buddha thought that idealism is human thought in its first stage, based on a subjective viewpoint. But as a reaction to this first stage, materialistic thought arises naturally. These two viewpoints are always in conflict; a fact which can be seen in every country in the civilized world. Gautama Buddha established Buddhism to transcend both idealistic and materialistic thought. Buddhism synthesizes the idealist's point of view with the materialist's point of view to give a realistic viewpoint. To achieve this synthesis and to realize Buddhism, he recommended us to practice Zazen.

I believe that this series of philosophical viewpoints; that is, idealism, materialism, realism and reality represents Buddhism's most important theory, a theory which can be used by people everywhere as a way to look at and regulate their life and their role in society.

A concrete example of an idealist is a person who is always suffering from the frustration of being unable to reach his ideals. A materialist suffers from being unable to find any meaning in his life beyond the pleasures of the senses. We can say that the idealist would do well to study the world around him through his senses, and the materialist would benefit from becoming a little idealistic. In this way, both of them can find a synthesis between the two states, and this is the Buddhist state. When people find the realistic attitude to living which Buddhism advocates, they can think, feel, act and live in a realistic way themselves. This will make their lives more satisfying than the life of an idealist or a materialist.

In the area of science, Buddhism believes in harmony between science and religion. Until the end of the Middle Ages, spiritual religions had a very powerful hold. But in modern times, belief in spiritual religions has become weaker and weaker, defeated by the discoveries of modern science. This is not a stable situation. Of course, scientific knowledge is vital to our lives. But it should not lead us to deny what has yet to be discovered by science. Most people do not appreciate this fact; they think that it is not consistent to believe in both science and religion.

Buddhism gives us a very good solution to this problem: in the Buddhist *Theory of Four Views*, spiritual religion is the first step in the progress of human thought, and science is the second step. In the area of intellectual thought, these two stages are fundamentally contradictory. But Buddhism says that these two stages are only different faces of one and the same reality. There is no fundamental reason why a scientist cannot believe in a religion too. The Buddhist viewpoint is that people should search for a new religion which is not contradictory to the beliefs of science. Considered realistically, it is possible to find a belief which synthesizes spiritual religion and scientific truth. This belief is a new religion. To establish this new religion, we practice Zazen.

In our everyday life, the *Four Views* can be of great help in solving real problems. For example, supposing as a businessman we want to build a new factory. If we first study the project on a theoretical basis, from other people's reports and reference books, we will get an image, an ideal image of our factory as we want it to be. If we were to go straight ahead and build our factory based only on our idea, we would probably fail. This is because our ideal image of what we want does not fit the real situation.

We should move on to a more objective and practical consideration of the problems involved. How much will the land cost? What about water and electricity supplies? What is the labor situation in the area? What is the average wage in the area? How can sufficient capital be raised? The answers to these practical questions will give us a more realistic picture of our project.

With our image and our practical consideration we can now move on to make a realistic plan of action; a synthesis of our original idea and our concrete research. Our action plan may be far from our original idea. But it is probably the most practical plan which has a chance of working in practice. At the same time, it is only a plan; it is not the factory itself.

In the end, we have to make a move; we have to step forward and start to build our factory. When we do this, we find that the real day-by-day work is completely different from our plans, and presents many unforeseen problems. This is because even our carefully researched plan still belongs to the area of thinking. The factory we are building belongs to the real world. In the real world we have to go through many trials and troubles. And it is through these trials and errors that the real factory is slowly constructed. The series of phases in the project; the idealistic phase, the objective phase, the planning phase, and the practical phase itself always exist in our daily living.

When we have recognized the necessity of this series of stages in our thinking, we can usually be successful. Without being aware of this progression through the four stages, those who are very idealistic will sometimes fail because of their strong and often brave ideals. And those who are too objective with no ideals will also fail because their objective analysis of all possible pitfalls will make them too cautious. They may hesitate through fear of failure. Some people then, are too brave, too idealistic. And others are too cautious, too objective. To avoid being too brave or too cautious we practice Zazen.

In the *Shobogenzo* Master Dogen says, *"To practice Zazen is the whole of Buddhism, and Buddhism is just the practice of Zazen."* So from the ultimate viewpoint, practicing Zazen is the aim of our lives. Zazen is not just a way of finding success in our life, it is enlightenment itself. To practice Zazen is the Truth itself. The practice of Zazen allows us to bring our ideals, objectives and realistic plans together into one synthesized whole.

CHAPTER TWO
SPIRIT IN BUDDHISM

CRSO

BUDDHISTS BELIEVE IN THE UNIVERSE. The Universe is, according to philosophers who base their beliefs on idealism, a place of the spirit. Other philosophers whose beliefs are based on a materialistic view, say that the Universe is composed of the matter we see in front of our eyes. Buddhist philosophy takes a view which is neither idealistic nor materialistic; Buddhists do not believe that the Universe is composed of only matter. They believe that there is something else other than matter. But there is a difficulty here; if we use a concept like *spirit* to describe that *something else other than matter*, people are prone to interpret Buddhism as some form of spiritualistic religion and think that Buddhists must therefore believe in the actual existence of spirit. So it becomes very important to understand the Buddhist view of the concept *spirit*.

I am careful to refer to spirit as a concept here because in fact Buddhism does not believe in the actual existence of spirit. So what is this *something else other than matter* which exists in this Universe? If we think that there is a *something* which actually exists other than matter, our understanding will not be correct; nothing physical exists outside of matter.

Buddhists believe in the existence of the Universe. Some

11

people explain the Universe as a universe based on matter. But there also exists something which we call *value* or *meaning*. A Universe consisting only of matter leaves no room for value or meaning in civilizations and cultures. Matter alone has no value. We can say that the Universe is constructed with matter, but we must also say that matter works for some purpose.

So in our understanding of the Universe we should recognize the existence of something other than matter. We can call that something *spirit*, but if we do we should remember that in Buddhism, the word *spirit* is a figurative expression for value or meaning. We do not say that spirit exists in reality; we use the concept only figuratively.

Are there any questions?

Are value and meaning the same?

Yes. I use them to express almost the same meaning. *Spirit* is used as a figurative expression for value or meaning. Idealistic philosophies support a belief in the existence of spirit. Buddhist philosophy examines the Universe from two sides; the idealistic side and the materialistic side. So the two concepts of spirit and matter are convenient concepts to use when explaining the Universe from these two viewpoints. The word *spirit* is used to mean value or meaning.

How is spirit manifested in Buddhism?

The straight answer is that Buddhism does not believe in the existence of spirit. The Universe is usually thought of as being composed of matter. But it is not only matter; there is also the value in our civilizations and cultures which arises from matter. Matter is one concept to explain what the Universe consists of. But Buddhists consider that the Universe is ultimately ineffable; that is, beyond description.

What do you mean by the value of matter?

Matter has physical or economic value, but this is not the ultimate value that matter has. The ultimate value of matter is its value to human beings. For humans, eating is very important. But it can never become the ultimate aim of living; we cannot live just for the purpose of eating. Although we eat every day, we are not satisfied with just eating. Our life depends on another value which is not economic or physical in nature. Although economic or physical value is the basis of all civilizations and cultures, matter gives rise to another value besides its physical value.

You mean human beings cannot be satisfied with just physical value every day, so there must be some other value?

A rather nice way to explore the meaning of *value* is to look at the history of human civilizations. For thousands of years, human beings have made their efforts to build something. It is extremely difficult for us to describe clearly what that something which we have been striving to create is. But looking back at the history of the last few thousand years, we can see that the something which we have made can be called *value*.

You say that Buddhists don't believe in spirit as something different from matter. But what is the difference between what you call 'something' and what someone else calls 'spirit'?

My *something* is included in the Universe. When we look at the Universe from one side, we see its spiritual face. When we look at it from the other side we find its material face. So it is not possible to prove that spirit really exists or that matter really exists. And those who insist that the Universe is only matter lose one face of the Universe. Idealists who say that the Universe is spirit do too. Both these ideas are incomplete. And in that respect they are wrong. In Buddhist philosophy we believe in something other than matter; matter is only one face of the Universe. We have another side with no name. This is the situation. The existence of this other, nameless, face of the Universe can never be denied.

Is the reason that we do not call it 'spirit' or the spiritual face of the Universe because that belongs to the realm of metaphysics?

It is because the Universe is a unity. If we insist that spirit exists separately from matter, we easily fall into a wrong understanding of the Universe. So we avoid adopting that way of thinking. Buddhist philosophy says that the Universe is ultimately ineffable. Of course, we use the concepts of *matter* and *spirit* in our explanations. But they are only a means of explaining. They are not the ultimate nature of the Universe. Buddhism says we can believe in the existence of the Universe itself. This is fundamental to Buddhist thought.

Dogen uses the word 'mind' in the sense of spirit, doesn't he? Don't you think that mind is almost identical with spirit?

Well, 'mind' is another concept used in explaining; Master Dogen said in the *Shobogenzo* that mind is one eye with which to view the Universe, so he used the word in his explanations. But mind does not exist as a separate entity in itself. So Master Dogen said: *"The mind of eternal Buddhas is just fences, walls, tiles and pebbles."* This is a very important concept, and the words themselves are very well known. He did not affirm the existence of mind in itself. Mind only exists when placed against the external world. Mind and the external world can never exist as separate entities. This is the fundamental stance of Buddhist philosophy. So we can find the word mind used in the *Shobogenzo* as an explanatory concept.

Fundamentally, Buddhism believes in the unity of body and mind. When our body dies, we can find no trace of the mind. This idea is quite different from the Brahmanist ideas which were flourishing in India before Gautama Buddha. Still, many people find it difficult to distinguish between Brahmanism and Buddhism.

There is so much in the Universe that we cannot understand at the moment. But we will understand one day if we are able to change our way of thinking. This seems to me to be the basic problem...

I agree with you. We all have our own beliefs and our own religions. But religious ideas can never be absolute, because our ideas progress and change over thousands of years. But we can believe in some truth - we can believe in our own truth.

But isn't it possible that ideas in Buddhism will also change? As a religion gets older, it must change...

Well, I think that there are three kinds of religious beliefs; spiritual, material, and ultimately Buddhist. This is what I believe. I believe in this idea, and that is why I lecture on Buddhist philosophy. Everyone has the freedom to believe in their own religion. At the same time, however, we can find in history an evolutionary stream of religious development. In the early ages and in medieval times, people believed in spiritual religions. In modern times, we have come to believe in materialistic religions and science. But in the middle of the nineteenth century the history of religion entered a new phase. I think we are now looking for a third religion; one that is neither idealistic nor materialistic; a religion in the middle way; a religion of reality itself.

We are free to choose which religion we believe in from these three kinds. I selected Buddhism. I have no way of proving its absolute truth or otherwise, but I believe it is the ultimate truth. So I explain my beliefs to you. The situation relies upon belief. And the problem of belief is beyond the scope of discussion: I believe this - you believe this - another person believes that. This is the situation. If you say that you cannot believe my ideas, I cannot insist that you do. You have a right to your own opinion. Religious beliefs are bound by these factors. But I believe in Master Dogen's ideas.

But that was seven centuries ago! That's a long time...

Yes. But think of the light that we see from the stars: the light itself left the star billions of years ago. Compared to that scale of time, the difference in time between Master Dogen and ourselves is not so very long.

Yes, but sometimes the light we see is from a star that no longer exists...

So time is indeed very relative. But Master Dogen's ideas are very modern ideas. When I read the *Shobogenzo* for the first time, when I was a still a boy, I was astonished to find that it contained ideas which were almost too modern. After reading more, I began to believe in his ideas. And I have now studied those ideas continuously for more than forty years. And now I have no doubts about his ideas at all. So I think that the truth can overcome differences in time. The truth deserves to be studied.

If we believe in the Ineffable, can you explain why it is necessary to study the intellectual and material face of reality?

In the history of philosophy, two systems of thought have emerged; idealism and materialism. Idealists base their thoughts on the existence of spirit, and materialists base their thoughts on matter. To explain the third system of thought that Buddhism uses, we can make use of these two existing systems. So we study these two faces of reality.

Is it a process which must continue? For example, if someone believes in Buddhism, they read the words of Buddhism and decide that they will become a Buddhist. Is it then necessary for them to study the spiritual and material faces of the Universe?

Yes. It is a method of explanation. It is not essential to be able to explain, but the two philosophical systems allow us to understand and explain Buddhist theory. So we use the two systems as phases in our Theory of Four Views.

Did Master Dogen write the Shobogenzo in order to convert people to Buddhism, or for Buddhists who already believe in the Ineffable to read? Was he preaching to Buddhists or to convert people to Buddhism?

Master Dogen said that Buddhism is belief in the Universe, and that the Universe or Dharma includes all. Therefore Buddhism embraces the whole Universe. Thus Master Dogen believed that no-one can deny the truth of Buddhist philosophy. This was his belief. He did not try hard to convert other people to Buddhism. He believed that, because Buddhism is belief in the Universe, belief in everything, it is natural for us to believe in Buddhism, to believe in reality. This is the situation.

When I started to study Buddhism, I read a book by Shunryu Suzuki, a Soto priest. He seemed to be saying that the important thing to do was just to practice Zazen, and that to study idealism and materialism was not important. When I said this to you, you said that you disagreed with his opinion. I still don't understand why.

The reason we get involved in idealistic and materialistic thoughts about the world is because human beings like thinking. For thousands of years we have made great efforts to find the truth through intellectual thought. This is a fact. Human history has produced many philosophical systems. When we look at a problem, our tendency is to think about it. So the best way is to make use of our tendency to think in studying Buddhism. The use of philosophical ideas is only a means.

It isn't necessary, then?

No, it isn't necessary. That's true. If we practice Zazen every day, we need no philosophies; we need no theories. When we attain the truth, we can find how to live. Then we can find the aim of our own life, and make our efforts to reach that aim. So finding the fundamental basis of life is the most important task we have. That is why I urge you to practice Zazen and attain the truth.

But I think that we tend to think about the problem first, before finding that Zazen can help us.....

Well, I'll explain the situation in this way: Thinking, feeling and practicing Zazen all exist inside the Universe. And when we are practicing Zazen, we are experiencing the Universe from inside it. In comparison, intellectual thought looks at the Universe from outside it, as if distanced from it. And feeling is perceiving or receiving stimuli from the world outside us. So we have these three modes or attitudes in which we experience something which we call the Universe. But in fact it is impossible to say *the mind exists here*; it is even impossible to say *I am here* with any final certainty. *Something* is in existence, and so people say *this is my mind* or *this is me*. But these are only ways of explaining the existence of....*something*. We can never prove these ideas true or false. This is the real situation. In order to discover this fact, we practice Zazen. During Zazen, we are unable to find *mind* or *body*. We are just sitting - or rather, *something* is just sitting. In Buddhism situations of this type are called ineffable. So we say that the *something* is the Ineffable. We can say that practicing Zazen is looking for the Ineffable. It is certainly a very strange state of affairs, but it is the real situation in our life.

In Buddhism there is no self, so of course there is no mind. But you said that the Universe includes something which is not matter. At the moment of death, does that something also cease to exist?

No, I think that after my death the Universe continues its existence. I do not believe that after my death the Universe will end.

What about life before birth?

Buddhism affirms the situation in the present moment. According to Buddhist philosophy, it is impossible to discover the origins of this world. This is the fundamental attitude of Buddhism. So when Gautama Buddha was asked by his disciples whether there was a beginning to this world, he did not answer. He just smiled. This was his attitude, because he knew that such problems are beyond the intellectual ability of humans. The German philosopher Immanuel Kant also confirmed the same fact. He concluded that such metaphysical questions are beyond the ability of the intellect. Gautama Buddha knew this fact, and this was why he did not answer these questions. It is a very interesting attitude.

Do you think that Master Dogen was also very intellectual?

Yes, he was. But at the same time, he recognized the existence of a world other than that of the intellect. The value of Buddhism is in the fact that it discovered a world separate from the world of the intellect. People in modern times are very intelligent. They usually think that they live in the world in which their thoughts exist. But Buddhism suggests that another world exists besides the world of our thoughts. This is a very important point. So Master Dogen was very clever, very intellectual. But he also found another world. I think it may have been that because he was so intellectual he had to find another world in order to survive. In the same way, modern man is very intellectual. And so he needs to find the existence of a world other than the world of the intellect. This is the situation in today's world, I think.

If we don't practice Zazen, it's so difficult for us to find a standard isn't it?

Yes. Zazen teaches us everything. This is the situation. So to understand Buddhist theory is not the most important thing; to taste Buddhism is the important thing. That's why we practice Zazen.

There are different kinds of people; some are calm, and some are nervous. Would you suggest different things; for example, different lengths of time to practice for these different people?

The unfortunate fact is that only people who believe in Buddhism practice Zazen. This is the real situation. I urge you to practice Zazen, but you are free to decide whether you will or not. I sincerely recommend that you do.

Thank you.

CHAPTER THREE
SPIRIT IN BUDDHISM II

IN MY LAST LECTURE, I explained the Buddhist idea of *spirit*. I feel there was some ambiguity in my explanation and so I would like to explain the concept again. I think that the ambiguity arose from two points; one was that I said that Buddhists did not believe in the existence of spirit itself, but at the same time, I used the word *spirit* frequently. The second is that I did not make use of the Buddhist system of the four philosophies in my explanation. I think that it is impossible to fully explain Buddhist theory without making use of the logic of the four philosophies. So today I would like to explain the problem of the concept *spirit* using the four philosophies.

From the idealistic viewpoint, people believe that mind really exists. This is basic to idealistic philosophies. Idealists also tend to believe that spirit exists as an entity in itself. We can say that the concept *spirit* forms the center of idealistic philosophies. In Buddhism, the concept *mind* is used in explanations without any belief in the existence of mind, or spirit, as a separate entity. The concepts are used purely as a means of explaining the philosophical problems of this world. So Buddhists are not people who believe in the existence of spirit as an entity in itself. In the first stage of the logic of the four philosophies, the idealistic approach, Buddhism employs concepts like *mind* and *spirit* for the purpose of explanation, but denies the existence of spirit as a real entity.

From the materialistic point of view, people believe in the existence of matter. Materialistic philosophies are based on matter. But in Buddhism, matter is used as a concept to explain the world; Buddhists do not believe in the existence of matter as a separate entity in itself. Materialists explain *mind* as part of the physical world. But they do not support the existence of spirit. In the second, materialistic step of the logic of the four philosophies, Buddhists, too, do not believe that spirit exists.

From the third point of view, we consider the problem on the basis of real action and experience. Here, action is explained as contact between mind and the external world. Action cannot be divided into mind and matter. When we are acting, there is no time for us to consider whether action is divided into mind and matter or not. Thus in the third phase, there is no room for belief in the existence of spirit.

The ultimate viewpoint transcends all philosophies. We are living in the reality, and we rely on the practice of Zazen to keep us aware of this fact. By practicing Zazen, we experience the state in reality itself. And this experience of what reality is forms the basis of Buddhist belief. So in the ultimate phase, we believe in reality in this Universe. We can never prove that what we experience is reality; no words can explain the experience. Our only attitude to the existence of reality is simple belief. From this ultimate viewpoint, Buddhism is a kind of metaphysics, a kind of religion. To have this belief in the reality of the Universe is to be a Buddhist. We believe in the existence of reality, but we do not divide it into two parts; mind and matter, or spirit and form. Thus, in the ultimate phase, Buddhists cannot believe in the existence of spirit; we deny the existence of spirit.

Are there any questions?

The reality that forms the basis of your belief; does that reality form the basis of your belief after you experience it in Zazen, or is there belief before that?

The belief comes from Zazen, from the reality as experienced in Zazen. So practicing Zazen is the origin of the Buddhist's belief in reality.

Can you explain what psychologically or spiritually draws someone towards Zazen?

Yes. The original motivation for someone to start practicing Zazen is often a feeling that there is nothing of value in their life; nothing that can be relied upon. Such a mood in someone's life is one of the reasons why they may start to believe in Buddhism and start to practice Zazen. From that point, the experience of Zazen itself begins to provide the motivation.

I usually use the theory of the autonomic nervous system to explain the action of Zazen on our body and mind. The autonomic nervous system has two sub-systems; the sympathetic system and the parasympathetic system. These two systems are constructed to work in opposition. When there is a balance between the two systems, we feel peaceful. That is our natural state. But we usually live with some level of tension as the result of an imbalance in favor of the sympathetic nervous system. When we are working, we are usually in a state of tension. But that tension is not our natural state. If we want to live naturally, we should come back to our natural state. Practicing Zazen does this; it allows the two systems to balance, and so we return to our natural state. When we are sitting in this natural state, we can feel the whole Universe or reality with our whole body and mind. This is the meaning of Zazen.

Is the reality that one person perceives through practicing Zazen the same reality that another person perceives?

Yes. We can say that reality is universal. So we can call reality the Universe.

Then it is not relative to the human spirit?

I sometimes use the word mind to explain our experience, but, as I said, I don't like using the word spirit because it suggests that I believe in the existence of spirit itself. In Buddhist philosophy, mind is used to explain; some people use spirit with a similar meaning to mind, but I think the word mind is better in discussions of Buddhist philosophy.

Can you tell us something about the meaning of mind in Buddhism?

Mind is a kind of mirror which reflects the external world. In the third phase of Buddhist philosophy, the *philosophy of action*, mind is seen as identical with the external world itself. In other words, mind and the external world are one inseparable unity. But in the first phase of Buddhist philosophy, where we consider the problem from the subjective viewpoint, the concept of mind is used as a means to explain this world from the side of the subject. Sometimes mind refers to our consciousness, too. This is the Buddhist view.

Would you tell us about your experience in Zazen?

Okay, I will tell you what happens in my own case when I practice Zazen. At the beginning, I am usually thinking without being consciously aware that I am doing so. Then, after several minutes, I recognize that I have been thinking about something, ruminating if you like. I then start to make my efforts to stop my thinking. In this state, I am sometimes thinking, and sometimes not. These two states interchange again and again. Then, usually after about thirty minutes, I enter another state; in this state I do not need to make any effort to stop thinking. I am just sitting. It is a very comfortable, peaceful and natural state.

So first I am unconsciously thinking. Then I recognize that I am thinking. Then I start making an effort to stop thinking. Then, finally, I enter a state where I need not make any effort to stop thinking. These are the four usual states in my Zazen.

When you enter the final state, do you have any desire to return to the ordinary state?

The ultimate state is a very ordinary state. Coming back to this natural state is the aim of Zazen. The state we are in when we are thinking about something is not always our natural state. The fact is, the state in which we are acting is our natural state. This is the fundamental basis of Buddhist philosophy. We revere action itself.

In our daily life, our action saves us; when we are worrying about something, our state is not peaceful; when we are receiving stimuli from the world around us, we are not always happy. But when we are immersed in our action we are happy and at peace. This is a basic fact of life. So Buddhist philosophy says we should devote ourselves to action; it is the basis of Buddhism.

How does one translate one's experience in Zazen into one's daily life?

Do you mean, how can we enter the natural state when we are not practicing Zazen?

Well, if someone is very conscientious about practicing Zazen, both at home and at a temple, if we want to translate that experience as much as possible to times when we are not practicing.....

Yes. In practicing Zazen, the most important thing is regular daily practice. To practice Zazen every day, even for a short time, is the best way to make Buddhism real in our daily life. Even when we are very busy, we should find some brief period when we can practice Zazen. It is the fundamental starting point of Buddhist life.

But when we practice every day, is there anything we can do when we are not practicing Zazen to.....

Let me illustrate the situation with an example. When we practice Zazen first thing in the morning, our body and mind enter the natural state. So we eat our breakfast in the natural state. We work in the office in the natural state. We study and read in the natural state. After practicing Zazen, we can do everything in the natural state; it is the effect of practicing Zazen. So I urge you to practice Zazen regularly, every day.

You described your own experience in Zazen, and talked about realizing that you are thinking and starting to make efforts to stop. I think that, for someone new to Zazen, that effort sounds a bit mysterious. We don't know how to make efforts to stop thinking. How do we do it?

Do you need to make efforts to stop thinking in your Zazen?

I think so, but the technique.... I usually think that there must be some way to do it. When you say "make an effort", I don't know exactly what kind of effort you mean. How do I not think?

During Zazen, I usually have some images in my mind, and these are a kind of thinking. So when I recognize that there are images in my mind, I make efforts to get rid of them. Do you have images when you are practicing Zazen?

Yes I do. But it's not the images which are the problem, it's that sometimes I don't understand how to get rid of them. Is there some particular method to get rid of them?

Well, I think that your state during Zazen is very natural and peaceful. You have the natural state from the beginning of your practice.

But when you speak of making efforts to stop thinking, usually, if I make efforts to stop thinking, I think of something else. I think about making an effort, or my mind just flits from one thought to another. And actually I don't stop thinking at all. I just get involved in a different kind of thinking.

Well, in that case, I usually focus my consciousness on keeping my lower spine straight and vertical. I concentrate my mind on making my spine straight. This effort stops my thoughts.

So, in a sense, this is your method, your technique?
Yes, that's right.

I find that, if I don't remain conscious of the position of my body all the time, I become conscious later that my body has moved into the wrong position. So is it possible, after many years of practice, to no longer have to think about your body?

After practicing Zazen for many years, our muscles become more used to the posture. So we don't need to concentrate continually on keeping our posture right. But usually we need to focus our consciousness on keeping our spine straight vertically.

At the beginning, are we intentionally making an effort not to think? Is it possible to make an effort not to think at the same time as keeping your body in the right posture?

I think that concentrating on keeping our spine straight and vertical is the best way to get rid of our thoughts. This is my method.

I often hear people recommend us to concentrate on breathing during Zazen. If I concentrate on my back, my back starts to hurt. If I concentrate on my breathing, my body becomes more controlled.

Yes, some people recommend us to concentrate on our breathing; to watch closely how we are breathing. But none of my experience shows me that I need to regulate my breathing. My breathing is fortunately always smooth during Zazen, so I have no need to regulate my breathing. I do not know what the basis of the theory about regulating breathing is.

Some people recommend, in the same way that you say you are conscious of your spine, to be conscious of breathing. So it's not to regulate breathing, but just to focus the mind on breathing or to count our breaths.

I do not recommend the method where you count your breaths. This is a kind of thinking, and such thoughts disturb our practice of Zazen. When I need a deep breath during my practice, I take a deep breath. Once or twice is enough.

I do not understand what the third phase, the philosophy of action is.

The *philosophy of action* is unique to Buddhism. It cannot be found anywhere else in the history of philosophy. European philosophies embrace many splendid ideas on materialistic and idealistic bases, but there is no *philosophy of action*.

Gautama Buddha found that we are living in reality. Reality is not only the mental side of life, but also the material side. So he considered that to think about the basis of the world from only one side, whether it be the idealistic side or the materialistic side, was not sufficient. He found another viewpoint, another philosophical position; the *philosophy of action*. Action is contact between the mind and the external world. Using the concepts *mind* and *external world* we can explain the world, or reality. But reality is not only how it seems from the inside, and not only how it seems from the outside. To explain the real situation we need a third point of view, a third philosophical standpoint.

This third point of view is Buddhism's secret; it is the valuable thing about Buddhism. To find this third point of view, we need to study Buddhism. But the third point of view is still not reality itself; it is still a philosophy. So in the final, or fourth phase, we have reality itself. Not theory, but fact. It is, for example the practice of Zazen.

The third stage is explainable but the fourth stage is inexplicable then?

Yes. It is the nature of reality itself. Reality is ineffable. Recognition of the ineffability of reality is an important wisdom in Buddhism. People usually think that all things can be understood with the brain, but this is not true. Reality can never be explained in words. This is the fact and this is the wisdom of Gautama Buddha's teachings; to recognize that there is something which can never be explained in words. To understand this is to put philosophy in its true perspective. Philosophy and fact are different. Recognition of the difference is of great importance.

Sometimes I struggle with my thoughts during Zazen, but as I relax I get different thoughts, different insights than when I've been struggling intensively. When you practice Zazen, do you get different insights into the things that you have been teaching about the previous day?

No. In Zazen we have no understanding. We experience the reality. We feel something through our whole body and mind. It is not thinking; it is not understanding. It is a kind of feeling. It is experience itself. We are always conscious during Zazen, but that consciousness is not thinking, not perception. This is the ultimate state in Zazen. The state of mind during Zazen is difficult to describe; it is not consciousness, neither is it unconsciousness. It is the state of pure action. We cannot be sure if we are conscious or unconscious. This is the fact.

So let's practice Zazen again now. Thank you very much.

CHAPTER FOUR
MATTER IN BUDDHISM

CR&O

TODAY I WOULD LIKE TO TALK about the Buddhist view of matter. I explained the Buddhist view of spirit in my last lecture, and so I would like to move on to the second phase and explain matter from the Buddhist standpoint.

It is said that modern philosophy was founded by the French philosopher, Descartes. At the beginning of his studies, he took the position of doubting all theories and propositions. But in that position, he found one simple fact; he found that he was thinking. His philosophy starts from that one simple fact. His famous words, quoted in Latin, *'Cogito ergo sum'*, say *'I think, therefore I am'*. So according to Descartes' theory, thinking forms the basis of our lives. But at the same time, he believed in the existence of matter. His philosophy is based on mind or thinking but he also believed in the existence of matter. Thus his philosophy is known as *dualism*. And these tendencies in Descartes' philosophical thought have continued through to modern idealistic philosophies. For example, the efforts of the German philosopher Immanuel Kant, who is known for his work - Critique of Pure Reason, were concentrated on investigating the basis of reason or mind. He was an idealist. He posited the existence of matter, which he called *ding an sich* -

or things in themselves, but concluded that it is impossible for human beings to prove the existence of matter. Therefore his philosophy was also a kind of dualism, although he is commonly called an idealist.

We can find another stream in modern Western philosophical thought; that is, English empiricism. Empiricists believe only in what they perceive with the senses, which they call *matter*. The idea was taken up by the German philosopher Feuerbach, who went on to assert that the world consists only of matter, and that nothing other than matter exists. For this, he is called a materialist. After him came perhaps the most famous of all the materialists, Karl Marx. He explained all problems and events on the basis of materialistic philosophy.

I think a very nice method of looking at the Buddhist view of matter is to compare it with matter as seen by the materialists, and then to compare the two views. Materialists believe that the world consists of matter alone. But Buddhists believe in the Universe. If the Universe consisted of matter alone, then the materialists' theory would be right. But Buddhists do not believe that the Universe contains only matter; they believe that it has another face. For example, the many people we can find in this world are involved in the activity called work. And human beings normally work for an aim. To work for an aim is a human value. The value is not purely materialistic; it is also cultural. It is a particularly human value. So in addition to matter, the Universe also contains human value, or cultural value. Materialists, however, deny this fact, and insist that the world consists only of matter and material value. This belief is very misleading when we come to consider the meaning of our lives. So Buddhists insist that the world is not only matter; it contains something other than matter - human value.

In the book *Shobogenzo*, Master Dogen says that nature is Gautama Buddha speaking, and that the mountains are his body. He says that the sounds of water in the valleys are Gautama Buddha's voice. What he is saying here is that nature is not only matter; it also has some human value. This is the Buddhist viewpoint. Buddhists believe that matter is only one face of the Universe. Matter is one method we use to explain the Universe. So Buddhism insists that to say that the world consists only of matter is wrong.

Are there any questions?

Do I understand correctly then, that Buddhists believe that there is a positive value to human life?

Yes. Buddhists believe that there is value as distinct from matter. Buddhists say, for instance, that what sort of food we eat is not of the ultimate importance; rather our interest in eating is our effort to create something of value. Considering what sort of food to eat is not the aim of our life. To work for something is the aim of human life.

Then materialists are perhaps confusing the method with the goal?

Materialists base their thinking about the problems of life on logical analysis of matter. But their ideas limit all things within their concept of matter. Their analyses are very clear and rational, but from the Buddhist point of view, they have forgotten something very important in our lives.

When you say human value, when we start thinking of the opposite of matter, we think of cultural value like listening to beautiful music and things like that. What is the difference between that sort of cultural value and what you mean by human value?

I use human value and cultural value with the same meaning. I don't know which is the more suitable to describe the expression of value. I intend both phrases to have the same meaning.

What about intellectual value?

Intellectual value is one small part of cultural or human value.

My question is very similar to the first one. But I still can't understand what you meant in your reply. I cannot understand why Buddhism is different from materialism just because human beings have value or values. Is it because those values are associated with something spiritual?

No, I don't mean that. I mean that value is a result of some sort of mental effort. But I do not think that it is spiritual. Buddhism believes in the existence of the Universe, and materialists look at that Universe from one side only. They look at only one face of the Universe, and they call that face matter. They then conclude that the Universe must consist only of matter. But Buddhists believe that matter is only one face of the Universe. It is impossible to describe the whole of the content of the Universe with words, so in Buddhist philosophy we express the Universe with the word *ineffable*. Materialists make the mistake of limiting the Universe within the boundaries of matter. But matter is only one of the faces of the Universe. The mistake that materialists make is to take part of the Universe and mistake it for the whole.

What is the other side?

According to Buddhist theory, the other side cannot be put into words. This is why we practice Zazen. While we are practicing Zazen, we can feel something. And that something is the other part of the Universe. So the Universe is sometimes simply called reality. And reality includes impossibly many facets. So we are unable to explain this other face of the Universe with words. This is the Buddhist view of the situation.

The word *inmo*, from the Chinese, is used to express the ineffable. This word has a very ambiguous meaning, because reality is very difficult to put into words. In Buddhist theory it is said to be impossible to explain the Universe itself in words. But by practicing Zazen we can experience this Universe. And this real experience is the only way we have of recognizing what the Universe is. We can explain it in philosophical terms, and in scientific terms, but these explanations are always one-sided. So if we want to grasp the Universe totally, we need to experience it with our action. This is why we practice Zazen.

Do materialists deny the possibility of any kind of human value, or do they just evaluate that value on the basis of materialism?

Materialists believe in material value. That is; energy, power, calories, and so on. But these are only material values. We cannot say that to get these kinds of value can be our life's aim. We make use of that which we perceive to be matter in our everyday life, but we make use of it in order to get some value which is not material. This is the fact. If we believe that getting material values like money, power in society and so on, are the aims of life, then we will lose the ability to see the real aim of life. This is the Buddhist standpoint. For example, take those people who put all their effort into getting rich, who love eating, and so forth. Even if they live in a gorgeous house and are surrounded by everything they want materially, they will find that sometimes they feel unsatisfied. This is simply because the things which they made the aim of their life - money, food, sensual pleasures - can never provide an ultimate aim for living. This is life's secret. And so Buddhism insists that although we need material things as a means to attain our ultimate aim, those things in themselves can never become that aim. Materialistic philosophies recognize only material values. They say that to make our societies better we need political power and to get political power we need revolution. This is their theory of society. But the Materialist's view of value and the Buddhist's view of value are different.

I get a little confused because you talk of materialists, but those materialists are being idealistic, and if the materialist has a philosophy, then that philosophy itself is an idea.

Yes. We can say that philosophy is ideas. But materialistic philosophies are based on matter - they analyze societies from a basis in matter. Their conclusion is that in order to govern a society it is imperative to control the means of production. So they strive to wrestle power over the means of production from the ruling classes, the bourgeois. Of course, their theories are ideas, but those ideas are rooted in matter.

Then, when a materialist is looking at the world, in reality, that person must experience human value, even though they may not realize it. When they do something, they must get some human value from their action.

Materialists do not generally believe that human societies can improve gradually. They believe that the situation is always controlled by the class with the greater power. They think that in order to improve society, we must defeat the ruling class. They insist on the absolute necessity of revolution. But Buddhist philosophy says that situations are changing at every moment, and so to live our best at the moment of the present is actually the best way to improve our societies. Buddhists believe that living our lives sincerely each day is gradual revolution. We do not need drastic revolution, because when we live our lives sincerely at every moment, our societies must be improving at every moment. This is the theory of Buddhism, and it is different from the insistences of materialists.

Generally materialists believe that the Universe is predictable, and Buddhists believe that the Universe is unpredictable. Can you explain what Buddhists believe causes this unpredictability?

In the second phase, Buddhism affirms materialistic ideas,

and so Buddhists also believe in the rule of cause and effect. So we also believe that the future is predictable. But at the same time, Buddhists believe that life is instantaneous - that time between present and future is discontinuous. So even though Buddhists believe that the future is predictable, we also believe that these predictions are only predictions, not fact. So Buddhists believe that the future is knowable, but they do not rely on this knowledge as absolute fact.

I can never understand how, if you believe in cause and effect, you can at the same time believe in human freedom.

To solve that problem, you need to understand the Buddhist view of time. In Buddhist philosophy we think about time in two ways. In one way, we say that time forms a continuous line from past to future. But at the same time, Buddhism is a very practical philosophy, which is based on action - action which takes place at the moment of the present. So even though we can imagine a long line of time from past to future, we believe that real time is just the moment of the present. This is the fundamental Buddhist theory about time. Buddhists believe in the rule of cause and effect; when we think of time as a long line, we can find the rule of cause and effect operating.

But if we believe solely in the rule of cause and effect, we must become determinists; we can never believe that human beings can be free. Buddhism also believes that the only real time is the present moment. This moment has no length; and in the present moment with its zero length, we can find our freedom. A rather good simile is a pea balanced on a razor blade: because the blade is very thin, the pea has an equal chance of falling either side of the blade. Human freedom has the same basic character. Because our action is at the infinitely short moment of the present, it sometimes goes one way, sometimes the other.

This is the Buddhist view of human freedom. And this theory allows us to reconcile the rule of cause and effect with belief in human freedom. In western philosophical thought, belief in the rule of cause and effect does not allow for simultaneous belief in human freedom, and vice versa. This is a well-known and unresolved contradiction in western philosophy. No-one has found a solution to this problem through the thousands of years of philosophical development. But Buddhism has a theory which can reconcile these two: belief in cause and effect and belief in free-will. So the Buddhist theory of time is very important; we call it *The Instantaneousness of the Universe*. Buddhist theory states that the Universe appears and disappears at every moment; time is fragmented or discontinuous. Only the moment of the present really exists. And it is this theory of time which allows the contradiction between free-will and cause and effect to be resolved.

If we believe in the instantaneousness of the present moment, and we are acting sincerely, why is it necessary for us to believe in a rule of cause and effect?

It is because we have the ability to think about our predicament with our intellect. When we consider problems on the intellectual level, we must acknowledge that there is a law governing our actions, the rule of cause and effect. This rule enables us to understand and make sense of the real situations in our lives. But at the same time, this rule can never explain the whole story; we need to look at life from another point of view besides the deterministic viewpoint of causality. Buddhism encourages us to look at life and the way the Universe works in many different ways. The rule of cause and effect is one of these ways; one way to explain the Universe.

I think that Zen is not definite about the validity of causal law; there is a part of the Shobogenzo where a priest asks which is correct, causal law or freedom.....

To fully understand the relationship between human freedom and the rule of cause and effect, we should use the *Theory of Four Views*. From the first viewpoint, we can believe that human beings have complete freedom, because this viewpoint looks at reality with the mind's powers. The second view is that the Universe is governed by cause and effect, because this view looks at reality from the external, objective, and material point of view. These two viewpoints - freedom and causality - are contradictory. To solve the contradiction, Buddhism has a third viewpoint - the *philosophy of action*. This is the philosophy of the present moment. The Buddhist theory of time states that the Universe is instantaneous. This theory enables us to say both that we are free at the moment of the present and that we are bound by cause and effect. To realize these three viewpoints, we practice Zazen, because during Zazen we can experience what reality is actually like by sitting quietly. So to realize the validity of the *Theory of Four Views*, we need to act, to experience something real. And practicing Zazen gives us this experience in a very simple and straightforward way. So now its time to practice Zazen once again. Thank you.

CHAPTER FIVE
ACTION IN BUDDHISM

────────────── ᘓᑄᔇᓌᑀ──────────────

TODAY I WOULD LIKE TO TALK about the "philosophy of action". I imagine that when people hear this phrase, they must wonder what it means!

In previous lectures, I have explained the meaning of mind and matter in Buddhism, and the Buddhist attitude towards idealistic and materialistic philosophies. When we hear about idealism and materialism, we can understand what they are quite readily because we can find so many examples of idealistic and materialistic philosophies in Western thought. In ancient Greece, we can find the philosophies of Plato and Aristotle, who are said to belong to the idealist school of thought. At the same time, we can find the philosopher Democritus, who was a typical materialist.

In medieval times, we can find theologies of Christian origin dividing into two distinct streams; realism and nominalism. In modern terms, nominalism belongs to the materialist school, and realism belongs to idealism.

In the recent history of Western thought, we can find many examples of both idealist and materialist philosophers; the idealists, Kant and Hegel, for example. Or Feuerbach and Marx, who are materialists. When we think about why these two philosophical schools dominated all else in Western thought, we must reach the conclusion that, when we consider the human condition with the intellect alone, we have to be either an idealist or a materialist; there is no other choice. We can say that human beings are able to think about philosophical problems only from one of these two viewpoints. This seems a natural conclusion when we remember that we normally think about a problem in our minds first, as a mental proposition, before examining it in relation to the external world of matter. The human tendency to give value to the intellect usually means that we consider problems first idealistically, then materially.

When we experience an area outside of the area of thought or intellect, a whole new world appears. This is the external world, or the world of matter. So we can classify two distinct worlds; the world of the mind, and the world of matter. This is the way we tend to view the world from our mind; we feel that there is a mental world inside our heads, and a physical world outside. Western civilizations are highly intellectual and there have emerged two distinct and excellent philosophical systems based on these two views; idealism, and materialism.

But at the same time, these two philosophical systems are doomed to always be in conflict with one another. And the human race has been searching for an answer to this conflict for thousands of years. But it has proven impossible for philosophers to find a way separate from either idealism or materialism which would enable them to consider the problems of our lives from another non-conflicting point of view. So the human race has been suffering the effects of the conflict between idealism and materialism and has been unable to find a solution.

This very same conflict existed in ancient India. The idealistic religion of Brahmanism and the materialistic teachings of the Six Non-Buddhist Teachers were always in disagreement. This situation became clear to Gautama Buddha, and he worried. He worried how human beings could ever find a solution to the constant conflict - how they could ever find a peaceful state in which to live their lives. The fundamental problem is that inside our heads, we can be convinced that our ideas are the truth - or conversely, that our perceptions are the truth. It is impossible to prove which of these two positions is true; whether our ideas are always right, or whether our perceptions of the world are the reality.

Gautama Buddha found the solution to this age-old problem. He found the *philosophy of action*. The only clear explanation of the philosophy of action is to be found in a book written by the 13th century Buddhist priest, Master Dogen. I started to study the *Shobogenzo* as a young man, and at first could understand practically nothing. But after many years, having come to understand the *Shobogenzo* completely, I have also found out why it appears that the *Shobogenzo* is so difficult to understand - it is because the *Shobogenzo* is written about the philosophy of action. The philosophy of action cannot be understood following our usual habits of thought, and so seems impossibly difficult. But if we understand what the philosophy of action is, we can solve the conflict between idealism and materialism. So today I would like to outline the philosophy of action for you.

In Western thought, we can find a specific method of reasoning known as dialectic. The Greek philosopher Plato used the method in many of his books by having a discussion between two people on the problem he wanted to expound. He found this method - this dialectic - very useful in presenting complex philosophical problems, as have many others right up to the modern philosopher Hegel. Hegel's use of dialectic is known as dialectic idealism. Karl Marx also used dialectic to explain materialism. His philosophical method is known as dialectic materialism.

Thus, dialectic reasoning has been employed to buttress the conclusions of both idealistic and materialistic philosophers. But I found in reading the *Shobogenzo* that dialectic can also be used to point to a solution to the idealism-materialism conflict. In the *Shobogenzo*, Master Dogen puts great emphasis and value on our actions - on what our real conduct is. Both idealistic and materialistic philosophies belong to the area of the intellect; they exist in our brains. But life itself does not exist as intellectual thought - it is very real. So to truly find what the meaning of our life is, we must leave the intellectual area. This is the secret of Buddhist philosophy. If we want to study Buddhism, we must leave intellectual thought behind.

To consider what our actions themselves really are, to consider practice and conduct, is very important in solving this conflict between idealism and materialism. This is the philosophy which Master Dogen lays out in the *Shobogenzo*. It is a philosophy based on our actions. Action is the meeting between mind and the external world. So in this sense, action is both subjective and objective at the same time. Idealism is the philosophy of the subject, materialism is the philosophy of the object and the philosophy of action is the philosophy of both subject and object. Action is the contact between the mental world and the physical world and so it exists instantaneously, always in the present moment.

We have a mental image of time as a line extending from past through present to future. But when we study what action is, we are always dealing in the present moment. So the time of action is *now* and its location is simply the place where we are at this moment - *here*. In the *Shobogenzo* Master Dogen uses the Chinese word *shali* to suggest this place, and the Japanese word *nikon* to express the present moment. He constructs his *philosophy of action* on the basis of the here and now. He explains that our life is not only a mental experience, not only a physical experience, but something real in itself.

When we examine philosophical problems from an intellectual point of view, we find it impossible to find any solution to the conflict existing between the idealistic or spiritual point of view and the materialistic or scientific point of view. But Master Dogen uses the dialectic method to synthesize these two differing viewpoints. It is impossible to explain the philosophy of action without using both of these opposing viewpoints; we need both idealism and materialism. We also need the dialectic method.

In short, if we look at problems from both the idealist's and the materialist's point of view, and then use the dialectic method to synthesize the two opposing views, we can find the philosophy of action. Then we can understand the true meaning of our life. So if we want to understand the philosophy of action, and if we want to realize the Buddhist state, studying idealism and materialism in Western thought is of central importance. To understand the real meaning of life, we need the philosophy of action. To find what this philosophy is, we need to use the dialectic method to unite the opposing views of the idealist and the materialist. This is the reason we study the *Shobogenzo*; to study what the philosophy of action is, and to use it to solve the problems of our lives as Buddhists.

The *philosophy of action* seems a strange concept to people in the modern world, but understanding it can help us to understand the true meaning of our lives.

Are there any questions?

What do you mean by the dialectic method?

Some idealists believe that *spirit* really exists; that if our spiritual being is cared for, we will always be happy. But in the real world, although we may take care of our spiritual side, if we do not have food to eat, we will not be happy. Others find that they cannot believe in the supremacy of the spirit; they take a materialistic view of reality; they believe that *matter* is the basis of the real world. So some believe in the supremacy of the spirit, and others believe that matter is the root of everything. These two viewpoints can never meet. There is no compromise between the two.

But if we think about the problem from the realist's point of view, if we have nothing to eat, we cannot continue to live. But when we eat something to satisfy our hunger, we feel better, and we may then feel something which people call *spirit*. So considered purely from the academic point of view, there is no answer, but considered realistically we find that the dilemma is resolved in the course of our day-to-day lives. We have to work to eat. At the same time, eating of itself cannot become the aim of living. We look for value in what we are doing. Eating will not give us that value, that aim. But unless we eat, we can never arrive at our aim of achieving something of value. Reality is not wholly spiritual, neither is it wholly material. In living, the most important thing is neither spiritual in nature nor material. The most important thing is the reality in which we live itself.

The supposition that there is something called *spirit* is a thesis. The denial of the thesis that there is something called *spirit* is antithesis. A realistic viewpoint is the synthesis of these two viewpoints. We can make a similar supposition, denial, and synthesis about the existence of *matter*. The triangular relationship between thesis, antithesis, and synthesis is dialectic. In western philosophy, Plato, Hegel and Marx all used the dialectic method. The method is very useful in looking at philosophical problems.

For example, everyone has a conflict over morals in their life;

what is good and what is bad. Morals are at the thesis stage. They are ideals which we should try to attain to make life good. But morality alone cannot make societies good. In real societies, people are not always good. The conduct of many people is bad, and so societies make laws. People who break the laws are punished. Laws are the antithesis to morals; they bind us with no freedom. But if societies are governed too rigidly by laws, we lose our human dignity; we have no freedom in which to follow our moral code. The policy of a society synthesizes morals and laws. Individuals are free to select their own representatives, and those representatives make the laws. So social policy allows people freedom while at the same time allowing society to be maintained in a peaceful manner.

We can use this triangular dialectic method to look at all philosophical problems. And using it allows us to solve the conflict between the opposing views of idealists and materialists. Idealism constructs the thesis. Materialism makes the antithesis. And the philosophy of action explains how to synthesize the two sides. This is the relationship between the three viewpoints, and the meaning of the dialectic method.

How do we find that third viewpoint? Why can't I put another philosophy in the third place?

In order to get rid of intellectual thinking, we need to act, to experience something. Buddhism tells us to practice, to experience. This is why Buddhism recommends the practice of Zazen. With practice and experience, we can find another area besides the intellectual area. This is the secret that Buddhism holds. This is why we practice Zazen.

You say that the dialectic method is a triangular method of thinking. But it is difficult for me to understand where the third point emerges. Is dialectic method the process to arrive at the third point?

47

We need four viewpoints. We can illustrate this with a diagram. First we have idealistic philosophies. And existing on the same level we have materialistic philosophies. We use the dialectic method to reach the third philosophy, the philosophy of action. But all three of these philosophies belong to the intellectual area. We need idealism and materialism to arrive at the philosophy of action. This is because the philosophy of action comes out of the conflict between idealism and materialism, using the dialectic method.

But reality itself exists outside of the area of the intellect, in a different area from any of these three philosophies. But using the three viewpoints, the three philosophies, we can suggest the existence of the world itself which is outside of the intellectual area. This is why Buddhism uses the four viewpoints to explain reality. So, in summary, we can use the two fundamental philosophies of idealism and materialism to enter into the philosophy of action with the help of the dialectic method. Then using these three viewpoints, we can reflect something which is different from any of those three viewpoints; that is, reality itself. We can never capture reality completely with our intellects. But we can suggest reality with the three viewpoints.

However, that suggestion is still not reality itself. This is why we need to practice Zazen. When we are practicing Zazen, we are sitting in reality itself. This experience is very important in realizing the meaning of our life. This is the relationship between the four viewpoints.

In your explanation you say we move to the third stage by action, or more completely, by Zazen. You also called it reality. So haven't you moved to the fourth stage?

Yes. Zazen belongs to the fourth stage. The philosophy of action is an explanation of Zazen; it is not Zazen itself. Zazen belongs to reality itself. This is the relationship between the philosophy of action and reality.

I still cannot understand, because you said that we reach the third stage by action.

I said that the philosophy of action can be explained with dialectic thinking using the two fundamental philosophies. But this explanation still belongs to the area of the intellect; even the philosophy of action is only a philosophy - it is not reality. But it can suggest the existence of reality and so, by studying the philosophy of action we can find the will to practice Zazen.

CHAPTER SIX
ACTION IN BUDDHISM II
ભ૭૪૭

TODAY I WOULD LIKE TO TALK more about the "philosophy of action" and its relationship with the two fundamental philosophies of idealism and materialism. I explained the relationship between the three philosophies and the dialectic method in my last lecture. But the theory about the dialectic is rather difficult to understand, so I would like to explain the philosophy of action again today.

The method of dialectic is indispensable in explaining the *philosophy of action*, so let me first give a more detailed explanation of what the dialectic method actually is. The word *dialectic* comes from the Greek words *dia* meaning two and *lect* meaning discussion or argument. So *dialectic* originally meant a discussion between two people. It suggests that the result of a discussion between two people gives a conclusion which is neither wholly the opinion of one of the participants, nor wholly the opinion of the other. Because of this simple fact, philosophers think that discussion allows the participants to reach new ideas which were not previously held by either party.

Dialectic method existed in Greek philosophy. The most famous of the Greek philosophers using dialectic method was Plato. He wrote many books containing discussions of philosophical problems. Plato used discussion as a way of presenting his own ideas. In this he was the first philosopher to use dialectic method. Then in the eighteenth and nineteenth centuries the famous German philosopher, Freidrich Hegel, used dialectic method very powerfully in explaining his theories. His philosophy is sometimes called dialectic idealism or dialectic spiritualism, because his ideas were based on mind or spirit. We can say he was an idealist.

Karl Marx, the famous materialistic philosopher also used the dialectic method. His philosophy is known as dialectic materialism.

I would like to use the example of a discussion between two people to illustrate the dialectic method for you. One party in the discussion is an idealist and the other is a materialist; let's call them Mr. I and Mr. M. When Mr. I and Mr. M discuss something, their opinions are always contradictory. For example, when they discuss the problem of morality, Mr. I explains morals on the basis of the conscience. This is the normal position of idealists. They say that if we listen to our conscience, our conduct will be right, and so they say that the existence of our conscience determines our morality or lack of it.

Mr. M on the other hand, does not agree that morals are a matter of conscience; he explains morals on the basis of circumstances and history. Materialists usually think that our conduct is determined by historical circumstances.

When we listen to the discussion between the two, we sometimes feel that Mr. I is right, and sometimes we think that Mr. M's opinion is the true one. In order to look at the discussion between the two people we really need a third person present. This third person will be able to reach a conclusion which is different from either of the two opinions being offered by Mr. I or Mr. M. This is how we reach the realistic viewpoint of Buddhism.

When Buddhists consider the problem of morals, they see the problem on the basis of our actions. Our actions are often led by our conscience, but at the same time, our actions are ruled to some extent by historical circumstances. So from the Buddhist point of view, the problem of morals is always a problem of how to act. Mr. I's opinion is partly true, but at the same time, Mr. M's standpoint is also true too because action contains two factors; one is our conscience or our intention, and the other is the circumstances. Action is always a synthesis of conscience and circumstances.

Buddhists give value to both these factors, because the way we act in reality is determined by both factors. For a Buddhist, morals are our actions themselves. The way that we act determines our morality or lack of it; not the way that we think alone, nor the external circumstances alone.

The method used in this short discussion above is the dialectic method - a method which synthesizes opposing viewpoints to reach a third point of view. The philosophy of action is constructed based on this method of thinking. It is a method which relies on two opposing opinions to form a synthesis of the two as a third and radically new viewpoint.

In ancient India, there was a typical idealistic philosophy called Brahmanism, and existing in opposition to it there was also a materialistic school of thought based on the teachings of six non-Buddhist teachers. Gautama Buddha was able to synthesize these two opposing philosophical systems into the philosophy of action. And so the philosophy of action became the center of Buddhist philosophy; to understand Buddhism it is necessary to understand the philosophy of action.

Are there any questions?

If we understand the philosophy of action, does that change our actions?

Yes. It can change our actions because when we understand the philosophy of action we can transcend idealistic and materialistic philosophies and follow the philosophy of action in our everyday lives. Understanding the philosophy of action has the power to change our conduct. At the same time, we should be clearly aware of the difference between ideas about action and action itself. The philosophy of action is an idea, and although we may understand the idea, sometimes our physical body is unable to move following the philosophy of action because we fail to realize that the philosophy of action is not action itself. So we can say that it is important for us to understand the philosophy of action in living a daily life based on Buddhism, but at the same time, we also need the practical ability to act following the philosophy of action. To get this ability to act, we practice Zazen. By practicing Zazen, we can get the ability to act following the philosophy of action. This is the relationship between our conduct in daily life and the philosophy of action.

If we don't study the philosophy of action, but simply practice Zazen, is our action different?

In practicing Zazen, we can experience action itself. So although our ideas are not formulated into a philosophy as such, we also experience the philosophy of action. With our modern life based on intellectual analysis, it is important to also have some systematic process by which to explain our experiences. But even though we may have no formal understanding of the philosophy of action, we can lead a Buddhist life. At the same time, when we also understand the philosophy of action, it is easier for us to follow the theoretical teachings of Buddhism.

The discussion between Mr. I and Mr. M is very familiar; the situation in which we sometimes feel Mr. I is right and sometimes Mr. M is right, such a feeling of uncertainty is familiar to me. But I rarely go beyond such a feeling of uncertainty and I can't find the point of synthesis in my own thinking. So I wonder if you have any advice about what to do when we come to such a situation in our usual life?

Yes. We should recognize that these two ideas belong to the intellect and that action is real. We are usually disturbed by the conflict between the two ideas, but in our real life, when we act, we throw away the disturbance. We can transcend the contradiction between the two ideas in real life by acting. This is the secret of our lives, and this is the secret of Buddhism itself. So acting saves us. This is Gautama Buddha's wisdom. When we transcend intellectual conflict by acting, we enter into a different world from the area of the intellect. In this situation, we can find a philosophy which is different from idealism and materialism. Synthesizing two intellectual philosophies means acting; that is, entering another area than that of the intellect. We can transcend the intellectual area by acting.

I said that the philosophy of action is the center of Buddhism; of course the real center of Buddhism is the practice of Zazen itself, because Zazen is the standard form of action. But the center of Buddhist philosophy is the philosophy of action. So Gautama Buddha told us to act. Action can save us. This is Gautama Buddha's teaching.

Can we understand that action is reached, not by rational thinking but by Zazen? How did Buddhists reach the third stage, action? By reasoning?

No. Practicing Zazen teaches us what action is. Practicing Zazen is studying action itself. The true meaning of action does not come from our rational thinking process; the experience of action can come only from acting.

In that case, there is no difference between the fourth phase and action?

We can say that the *philosophy of action* comes in the third of the four phases, and action itself belongs to the fourth phase.

I find that the word action is very difficult to think about. I tend to think that action means a certain type of action. Does action means just doing something? Could you explain it again?

Yes. It's a difficult problem and I don't mind explaining it again. We can describe the structure of the four philosophies as a triangular pyramid. First we can consider the starting point of our thinking to represent one point on the base of the pyramid. That is mind. With our mind, we enter the area of idealism. We usually think about philosophical problems intellectually.

But we can find that we are not only mind; we also have a physical body - we eat, we look at the world, we see colors, images; we hear the world. This area of perception - the realm of our physical body - can be represented by a second point on the base of the pyramid, giving us a line. The usual situation of our thought process finds us moving to and fro along this line as we consider problems from the contradictory viewpoints of idealism and materialism.

This line and the two viewpoints which occur on it belong to the area of the intellect. Our civilization is based on the human intellect. This is the reality of the modern world. Human beings progress and regress along this line between the two viewpoints. And in the same way, our civilizations also move to and fro; from idealism to materialism and back. These movements have created our civilizations. So the existence of these two contradictory points is very important. But for human beings, contradictory situations give rise to great suffering. This is because we have not been able to find a satisfactory solution to the contradiction. We have developed wonderful civilizations, but at the same time, the great suffering of the human race arises directly from these contradictory situations.

Sometimes, however, in our day-to-day life, we transcend this mental conflict by acting. For example, we may be reflecting on the misery of human life. But if we act - have a bath, eat something, go for a walk - we can rid ourselves of those painful thoughts. Acting enables us to transcend the contradictions in our minds. Action can help us. This is a very simple and obvious fact.

Gautama Buddha recommended us to practice a form of action; that is, Zazen. Because Zazen is a form of action, we can say that, just as Buddhism is based on the practice of Zazen, so Buddhist theory is based on the philosophy of action. Using the philosophy of action to think about a problem is to take our philosophical analysis out of the line on which the idealism - materialism conflict exists, and to add a third point to form a two-dimensional plane; one on which we consider realistic solutions. But even a realistic philosophy cannot save us, because in the end it is only the movement of electrical currents in our brain cells!

Philosophy can never be action. To realize what action is we have to transcend these three philosophies. And to do this we practice Zazen. The practice of Zazen enables us to find a solid, three-dimensional world. The three philosophies exist on a flat plane; Zazen, which is the standard of action itself makes our plane into a pyramid. To study real life, to study real action, we practice Zazen.

If we take someone like Hegel, did his philosophical position and his real life fit together?

Hegel started his philosophical exposition from sensory perception, which he explained from the point of view of the human mind. So his philosophical standpoint starts with the mind, travels to sensory perception and back again. His point of view oscillates along this line. He thought that he was using the dialectic method, but in fact he was only moving to and fro between the opposing points. This means that his philosophical thoughts and conclusions always remained in the intellectual area; he was unable to synthesize his views into a third realistic viewpoint. But people do not think it strange that his conclusions are in the area of the intellect. They think that it is perfectly natural for the conclusions to our thoughts to be thoughts themselves.

On the other hand, Marx starts his philosophical analysis from a materialistic standpoint. He explains the human mind on the basis of matter. This is diametrically opposite to Hegel, but nevertheless, Marx is also merely moving to and fro on the line between mind and matter. He also thought that he was using the dialectic method. Because Marx's conclusions were scientific and objective; based on the world of matter which we all perceive in front of our eyes, people feel that Marx's conclusions have a practicality which Hegel's conclusions lack - that Marx is objective. But in fact both Hegel and Marx left their philosophical conclusions in the intellectual area. Their conclusions were worked out theoretically, intellectually.

Gautama Buddha found a solid area; he found that action itself is the solution to the conflict. And the philosophy of action is the theoretical basis which suggests to us that the solution is outside of the area of the intellect. So Gautama Buddha's ideas differ from Marx's and Hegel's; Gautama Buddha constructed a solid where Marx and Hegel had built only a line on a plane. Using the four philosophies, we can create this solid construction for ourselves, and transcend the intellectual area in finding real solutions. To transcend the intellect is fundamentally important in Buddhism; without this transcendence, we will always remain caught in the solutions in our minds, even if we use the dialectic method. We will always be on the two-dimensional plane.

But in reality we are living in a three-dimensional solid area. This is a very simple fact which is very important to realize. We are living in the real world, which is not the same as the world of either our subjective or objective thoughts. To recognize this fact, we practice Zazen.

The theory I have discussed here is the "philosophy of action". It is rather difficult to grasp, but it is the center of Buddhism. So to understand Buddhism, we must understand this fundamental theory. We should transcend the area of the intellect and enter the world of action. We should act.

CHAPTER SEVEN
REALITY

_____ ⋘⋙ _____

IN THE LAST FEW LECTURES I talked about the three
philosophical systems; idealism, materialism, and the elusive
"philosophy of action". Today I would like to talk about the
ultimate phase of Buddhism. Of course there is a link between the
three philosophies so far discussed, and the ultimate phase, and it
is this link that I would like to explain first.

I explained that idealism is the first viewpoint in
Buddhism, and that materialism is the second. I then explained
how these two opposing viewpoints can be synthesized into a
third viewpoint, a realistic viewpoint. The philosophy of action
deals with this synthesis. These three basic philosophical
standpoints include all the philosophical systems in existence;
any philosophical system can fit into one or other of those
three basic categories.

Gautama Buddha was the first person to insist on a very
simple but very important fact; that we do not live according to
philosophical systems; we live in the real world itself. Although
this is a very simple and apparently self-evident conclusion,
many people in fact believe that the real world in which we live
is the same world as that world which we build up in our
heads, or that world which we perceive directly with our

senses. The vast majority of people living on the face of the earth take either one or the other of these two positions; that is, they either believe in idealism, or they believe in materialism. This situation is actually rather strange, but it is the fact.

The same situation exactly existed in ancient India. Gautama Buddha saw that this was the case, and he was able to recognize one simple fact clearly; that all people are actually living in the *real* world. He saw that people are prone to mistake the representation of the world that they build up in their brains for the *real* world itself, or they think that the world that they perceive with their senses is the only world that exists. Although this may seem obvious, people do actually believe that the philosophical systems they use to view the world are the world itself. Materialists believe that the world of matter as we perceive it is the complete world; idealists believe that the world is governed by ideas.

Gautama Buddha urged us to see the *real* world in which we are living; he said it was very important for us to realize this, and he dedicated his life to teaching people this simple truth. He said that to recognize that we are living in reality, it is necessary for us to transcend intellectual thought, whether it is based on pure ideas or on scientific theory, because both in fact belong to the intellect. Even the philosophy of action belongs to the area of the intellect.

Gautama Buddha used the Sanskrit word *Dharma* to describe the reality in which we all live. But he said that this reality is in the end impossible to put into words completely. We can give a good explanation of idealism or materialism in words, and we can even explain the philosophy of action. But reality itself defies description. This presents quite a problem. Gautama Buddha recognized this fact. He encouraged us to practice Zazen, saying that when we are practicing Zazen, we can recognize the reality that we are sitting in with our whole body and mind. He said that people who believe that the word of their thoughts is the real world are deluded. To free ourselves from those delusions is the aim of Buddhist practice.

When I show you how to practice Zazen, I usually say that there is no need to think about anything, and no need to feel any particular sensation during Zazen. When we are sitting in reality without thinking or feeling, we can recognize that very simple, primitive fact. And it is this experience that forms the basis of Buddhist philosophy. So to study Buddhism means to study reality; to practice Zazen is to study reality directly.

Such a direct and simple philosophy is very hard to find in this world. Usually, we try to solve the problems of life with our intellect alone. Almost all modern-day civilizations are based on the supremacy of the intellect. People are trying to live in the world of their ideas or the world of their senses. Buddhism teaches us the philosophy of action, which is itself a construction of the intellect. So to really know and experience the reality of this world, we need to practice Zazen. This is why Master Dogen said, *"Just practice Zazen. Practicing Zazen is Buddhism; Buddhism is practicing Zazen."* This is his teaching, and the center of Buddhism itself. When we recognize the nature of the real world, we can be Buddhas. To become Buddha means to recognize reality. This is the ultimate phase of Buddhism.

Are there any questions?

You said that materialism is also intellectual thinking. How is that?

Many people think that materialism is a realistic philosophy. But I do not agree. Materialism is a philosophy - and it is based on the concept *matter*. Materialists analyze all their problems from the basis of the concept *matter*. Although materialists think that matter is reality itself, it is only a concept invented by the intellect to explain that *something* we see or perceive out there. So their thoughts about the world spring from an intellectual conception of the world. That intellectual conception is not the real world itself.

When you say that most people think that the world of their thoughts, or the world of matter, is the real world, it sounds a long way from everyday life. The word 'philosophy' suggests a very grand and special sort of thinking. Can you give us a practical example? When we think that the world of our senses is the real world, what might we be doing?

The center of idealism is the mind. The center of materialism is matter. Matter is a concept which comes from the negation of mind. When we think about philosophical problems, we usually think about them either from a viewpoint based on mind, or one based on matter. People who consider themselves materialists have the concept of the real existence of matter as the basis to their thoughts. They are always conscious of the physical world around them. That's what I mean when I say that a materialist is living in the world of matter. But the idea that the world we are living in is composed only of matter as we perceive it directly with our senses is a kind of illusion; it is just an idea in our brain.

But when you say that someone thinks that they are living in a material world, as for instance, if I want to go and buy a new car or a new suit, what kind of thought is that?

In fact, we are all living in reality. But when we use our intellectual powers to make sense of our life, we usually become either an idealist or a materialist in our point of view. We all live in the same reality, but people tend to think about the meaning of their life. We usually find that our consciousness is attuned to one of two worlds; the world of our thoughts, or the world of our perceptions. The world which we perceive with our senses is not reality itself; it is a world viewed through a kind of conceptual framework. And in that way, it is a kind of illusion.

This is true equally of the world of our thoughts.

I understand your explanation on idealism and materialism. Plato was an idealistic philosopher. He stated that behind every building there must be the thought that produced the building first, in the architect's mind, for instance. This is not of matter. It is outside time and space and therefore holds a different reality to the materialistic world. My mind is fundamentally dualistic. I cannot conceive of unity with my mind. We think of something as black or white. That's one thing. The second thing is that my mind is conditioned by my past experiences. As reality must lie outside both time and space, and as my mind cannot conceive of anything outside time or space, I can only think of things in terms of past, present and future. Next, the conditioning. I, as a conditioned person, think with a conditioned mind. How can I be free from my conditioned mind? How can my conditioned mind understand reality? How will I get beyond my mind?

I would like to answer your first question. It concerns the dualistic nature of our understanding. Our dualistic understanding is a product of our intellectual processes; the intellectual faculty always divides and discriminates. This is its fundamental function. Without this fundamental capacity for discrimination, we are unable to think. So in considering philosophical problems, it is natural to divide; to discriminate. Our thoughts are always dualistic by nature. It is the fundamental nature of thinking. This is the first problem.

Your second question is about cause and effect. We need to understand the Buddhist theory of *Four Philosophies*. Gautama Buddha taught us that we are living in reality, and he said that in order to recognize this fact, we need to be free from the world of the intellect. To do this, Gautama Buddha said we should act. He said that we should act right. And to act right, he told us to practice Zazen. So his teachings are about morals or ethics; not moral or ethical problems as philosophy, but as problems of how to act, how to live practically. He said that to practice Zazen is the best way to be free from the world of our intellect and to act right.

By practicing Zazen, do you get an intuitive understanding of reality, rather than an intellectual one?

Yes. When we begin to practice, we enter reality itself at once. This is the situation. So Buddhist practice is a very easy way.

As a Catholic, I believe that the world was created by God. But at the same time, I believe in the existence of matter. I think that Buddhism is a kind of religion and a kind of philosophy too, but without a god. I think that the intellect is very important in Buddhism, not only in the sense of idealistic or materialistic thought. The intellect provides us with a kind of food; we must think, study and learn. Because we cannot realize reality without the intellect too. We cannot do it only by practicing Zazen. If you were to teach a little child only to practice Zazen without teaching it to do other things, the child would not grow. I think the practice of Zazen gives us one thing. We learn something new every day of our lives in this reality. But practicing Zazen is a kind of - how shall I say - our brain is a kind of computer which receives a lot of information every day. We are not able to use all the information in our computer without practicing Zazen. Without this practice, our computer does not work very well. It seems as if someone or something puts all the information in our brain's computer into the right place. And then, at the moment when we must act, we know how to act without thinking. It doesn't mean that we don't think; we think unconsciously. The practice of Zazen and enlightenment give us this possibility of realizing reality in the right way, without conscious thought.

I would like to say something about the relationship between God and the Universe in response to what you have said. Buddhism realizes the imperfect nature of the intellect. Many people believe that the intellect is absolute. But Gautama Buddha criticized this idea. He said that intellectual ability is not absolute. He urged us to recognize that we are living in reality. In Christianity, God governs the Universe. In Marxism, there is no God. Buddhists say that the Universe is God. This is a situation that we cannot recognize with our intellect. We experience this truth in our right action. Buddhists practice Zazen to experience that the Universe is God itself; God is the Universe. Buddhists do not believe that God exists outside the Universe. Furthermore, Buddhists deny the materialistic idea that there is no God. This is the relationship between three kinds of religions in the world today; Christianity, Marxism, and Buddhism. Which of these three religions we should select is an important problem for people today. But why must this be so?

Human beings have an inherent tendency to want to sacrifice their lives fighting for their beliefs. So idealists feel that it is worthwhile to lose their lives fighting against materialists. Materialists feel that to lose their lives fighting against idealists is worthwhile, too. This is the real situation in the world today. This tendency is inherent in the human psyche. It is a sad, but true, fact.

You said that our intellect is dualistic in nature. So why don't you include dualism along with idealism and materialism?

When we look at problems intellectually, our conclusion may sometimes be idealistic and sometimes materialistic. This is the unavoidable consequence of intellectual analysis. The intellect divides all things into black or white, good or bad, right or wrong. It is the way that our brain discriminates. So our thinking is inherently dualistic. But the Buddhist *philosophy of action* is able to synthesize these two sides, these two philosophical viewpoints. This philosophy of synthesis, however, is only itself a system of thought. Gautama Buddha told us to practice Zazen so that we could recognize the reality in which we live every moment. So in the area of the intellect, we are always dualistic. This is why there is no need to include dualism. The philosophy of dualism says that reality consists of two parts: mind and matter. But this suggests that both mind and matter really exist. The Buddhist viewpoint is that both mind and matter are concepts which exist in our brain; that reality is undivided. People who believe that mind and matter both exist as real entities are, from the Buddhist standpoint, deluded. Buddhists recognize the existence of a single undivided reality, a belief which comes directly from the experience of Zazen.

However, we need the idealistic and materialistic viewpoints in order to construct a philosophical system. Without both a right leg and a left leg, Buddhist theory cannot stand. Idealism and materialism are the legs of Buddhist theory. Reality itself cannot be explained in words, but because we human beings have the capacity and inclination to think about our lives and the reality around us, we need a philosophical system. The Buddhist philosophical system allows idealistic thought and materialistic thought to co-exist. But it does not believe that mind and matter are two real entities.

You said that the fundamental difference between Christianity and Buddhism is that in Christianity we have one God who is outside the Universe, and in Buddhism the creator and the created are one. So since God is everything, he is also you and me.....

I said that God and the Universe are united, but this itself is only a method of explanation. Buddhists do not feel it necessary to believe in the existence of some definite spirit or essence as an object. In Buddhist theory, we say that there is something which cannot be explained with words: the *Ineffable*. Some call it the Universe, others call it God, still others call it matter, spirit or soul. But in Buddhism, we say that the something which exists cannot be explained with words.

So what you mean is that we cannot know what the truth is because knowing is of the mind. We can only be the truth?

Yes. And we can experience it; we can act. We can practice Zazen.

PART II

NHK Radio Talks

Translated and Edited by
Yoko & Michael Luetchford

CHAPTER EIGHT
BUDDHISM AND ACTION
CRSO

TO BEGIN, I WOULD LIKE to give a brief description of what Buddhism is, the stream of philosophical ideas in world history, and the relationship between the two.

Buddhism is a religion that is based on training. The meaning of training here is practice and action, or "the practice of action." This is the distinguishing mark of Buddhism as a religion, and Buddhist theory has developed on this basis.

The nature of Buddhism as a religion based on action is of great significance if we look at the direction in which world history is pointing us. I would like to go into this in more detail, and with that aim, I would like to give a summary of the development of modern western civilization.

Civilization as we know it is believed to have started in Egypt, Mesopotamia, and India. Recent discoveries suggest that the oldest civilization in the world existed in Ethiopia. From there it spread outwards in many directions, arriving after a long period in the Aegean Sea area and on to the islands of Greece. In Greece the seeds of modern western civilization as we know it germinated, and modern civilization owes much to these origins.

From among the great thinkers of ancient Greece emerged

the philosopher Plato. He developed a philosophy which was centered on the rational workings of the mind, and which we call idealism today. The basic concepts of this new philosophy of idealism spread and were absorbed into the Roman Empire, from where they spread to the four corners of Europe together with Roman civilization. The time was ripe for idealism, and in the closing phases of the Empire, this idealism met the fledgling Christianity.

Idealism as embodied in the thoughts of Plato and Aristotle found a match in Christianity, with its belief in a perfect God living in Heaven, and one strengthened the other. Christianity was able to use the logical strengths of Greek idealism to develop a clear theology, and in turn, the ideals of Christianity came to form the center of a new set of philosophical ideals. The stage was thus set for Christianity to spread on the back of an idealistic view of the world throughout the length and breadth of European societies.

Christianity is a religion centered on belief in God, in whose image man is created. With this basic belief, the people of Europe created societies based on the Christian ideals which they held in their minds, and tried to live their daily life according to these ideals. This was well-suited to the times, when living conditions were poor, and belief in "salvation" provided the ideal escape.

At the end of the Middle Ages, however, productivity started to improve, and the life of people in Europe slowly improved. With this slow improvement in their standard of living, people began to realize their physicalness. Freed from the race for mere survival, they began to see that man has a physical existence. In short, a new way of looking at life slowly emerged.

Objective observation of the stars led Copernicus to the conclusion that the Sun was at the center of our Universe and that the Earth moved around the Sun. This was in direct contradiction to the Ptolemaic beliefs which Christianity supported at that time. But belief in the Copernican view of the Universe slowly took hold, and with it, the development of the first scientific theories. People had started to look at the actual concrete facts in front of them. In these conditions, science developed rapidly, and because of that development, accepted religious beliefs were broken down one after the other. This was unavoidable. European civilization entered a period of renaissance, a period in which society moved back towards a more human-centered existence, as in Roman and Greek times. With the Renaissance, a reformation in the Catholic Church also put a more human face on the nature of Christian belief.

At the end of the 18th century, the French Revolution was significant in breaking the belief in the divine power of kings, and this allowed people to start to see that with the creation of political systems people could govern themselves.

The 19th century saw a strengthening in the power of materialism, and with it philosophers like Karl Marx, who developed his philosophy that all things and phenomena in the world can be explained from the viewpoint of matter and material power. This ultimately led to a situation at the end of the 19th century in which the philosopher Nietzsche pronounced *"God is dead!"* By this he wanted to suggest that the power of spiritual religions had declined to the point where they were no longer effective as a basis for daily life.

But the big question is whether or not human beings can actually live without belief in a religion. To live without a belief is to live without an aim, without any criteria. In this situation, the question of the meaning of life is set into clear relief.

From the end of the 19th century and throughout the early part of the 20th century, a search started for something neither centered on religion, nor centered around the material world of science. Philosophers like Kierkegaard, Nietzsche, Jaspers, and Heidegger developed an existential view of the world, in which they declared that we exist at the moment of the present. The American philosopher John Dewey asserted his pragmatist views in which the criterion used to judge the value of something is not spiritual, not material, but is in accordance with its practicality: whether it is useful to man's life. Husserl went further with phenomenology and asserted that any discussions of the spiritual or material is useless. The essential thing is the way we view objects or phenomena as they appear in front of us. Wilhelm Dilthey's philosophy was centered around the human condition, denying both the spiritual and material realms.

These trends in the development of philosophical thought show us that people in the 20th century were not satisfied with idealistic beliefs centered on spirit, nor were they satisfied with the materialistic beliefs of science. This general dissatisfaction with current belief systems is still with us; perhaps the biggest problem facing mankind as we move into the 21st century is what belief system will we adopt as the criterion for civilization, what beliefs will form the basis of our societies in the future.

In this situation, I would like to suggest that we can look towards Buddhism, and I will explain why. Buddhism is not a spiritual religion, neither is it a materialistic system; it is a way of living based on action. The main characteristic of Buddhist philosophy is that it is constructed around the nature of action itself.

I will tell you why I say that Buddhism can form the basis of a new belief system for the world. When I was a student of 17 or 18, I became absorbed by a book called the Shobogenzo which was written in the 13th century by a Buddhist monk,

Master Dogen. For more than 50 years since then I have continued to study the Shobogenzo. During that time, reading it again and again, I translated it into modern Japanese. Going over it again and again to clarify the meaning, I have lectured on the Shobogenzo in different places probably more than 6,000 times. This long task has led me to see clearly that what Master Dogen is doing in the Shobogenzo is explaining the nature of reality. His explanation is centered on the nature of action. This has become very clear to me, and it has convinced me that the criteria for living that Master Dogen explains, based not on spiritual beliefs or material facts, but grounded firmly in our action, can form the basis of a new belief system, a new philosophy for the world.

Let me illustrate why I have come to believe this. There is a chapter in the Shobogenzo called Kajo, or Daily Life. In it Master Dogen quotes his own master, Tendo Nyojo:

*"The golden and splendid form
Is to get dressed and to eat meals."*

The *"golden and splendid form"* here refers to the figure of Gautama Buddha, who is said to have been surrounded by a golden aura. Master Tendo Nyojo's words mean that our daily actions of eating and getting dressed contain the golden splendor of the Buddha; that is, those everyday actions are splendid in themselves. This assertion contains the essence of Buddhism. But this essence is not just embodied in words and theory; it refers directly to our real actions in our daily life. Buddhism asserts that actions like getting dressed and eating meals form the very center of our real existence.

There is another chapter in Shobogenzo called *Jinzu* or Mystical Powers. This chapter discusses the nature of the special power that people get from Buddhist training. Master

Dogen quotes a Chinese man called Ho-on, who was a layman studying Buddhism while working in society:

"The mystical power and wondrous function,
Carrying water and lugging firewood."

This says that the Buddhist meaning of mystical power and wondrous function is contained in what in those days were the daily actions of carrying water and firewood. We drink water and use it for cooking. Firewood too was essential for cooking and for heating. So these two things were basic necessities of everyday life. What is mystical and wondrous about these activities is that they actually give life to us—they are our life itself. Looking at Buddhism in this way, we can see that it is not a religion based on something we create in our minds, it is a religion which teaches us clearly how to lead our lives day by day.

Let us now locate Buddhism in its place in the development of belief systems up to the present day. Spiritual belief was dominant in the Middle Ages, but has now given way to the power of materialism in modern times. At the end of the 19th century, people first started to lose faith in the ultimate power of materialism, leading to the current situation in which people are actively studying and sincerely seeking for an alternative criterion for living.

I sincerely believe that in this stream of history, Buddhism, with its basis in action, is at this time exactly suited to become the major belief system in the world. It has a philosophical system which can unify all others. This is my inescapable conclusion after my years of study of the Shobogenzo. You might feel, listening to my words, that what I am saying about the role of a theory based on the nature of action in the destiny of the world sounds too dogmatic—and this may be a natural first reaction. But I have studied the Shobogenzo since I was a young man, and what Master Dogen says about action and the teachings of Gautama Buddha leave me without a shadow of a doubt that the Buddhist belief system centered on action is destined to become the world's central philosophy.

At this point in time, mankind can no longer believe in mediaeval spiritual systems, and neither can it accept the supremacy of science in providing us with answers. The real situation is that people are searching with all their might. They are searching for something which is neither spiritual nor materialistic that they can rely on. In this situation it is inevitable for Buddhism to emerge as the central influence.

But what does action mean exactly? This is of central importance. In Shobogenzo there are many explanations of the nature of action. One example appears in the chapter *Shoaku Makusa*, or Not Doing Wrongs. A famous Chinese poet, Haku-Raku-Ten, is having a talk with his master, Choka Dorin. Haku-Raku-Ten was also renowned as a politician and was an enthusiastic student of Buddhism. After he had been appointed as governor of several districts in China, he became the student of Master Choka Dorin. One day he asked his master: *"What is the Great Intention of the Buddha-Dharma?"* Master Choka replied, *"Not to commit wrongs. To practice the many kinds of right."* Haku-Raku-Ten had hoped that his master would give him a scholarly and philosophical answer which would satisfy him. But Master Choka simply told him not to do wrong, but to practice the many kinds of right.

Haku-Raku-Ten was very disappointed with this simple and direct answer to his question, something as simple as not doing wrong, doing right! He said to his master, *"If this is so, even a child of three can say this!"* He meant that the answer was so simple that it could have been given even by a three year old child. He shows here that he thought that Buddhism was a far more sophisticated and philosophical pursuit, and not just consisting of simple expressions of conduct in our daily life. Master Choka replied to him: *"A child of three can speak the truth but an old man of eighty cannot practice it!"* Of course it is valid to point out that a three year old child can say don't do wrong, do right, but the point is that this admonishment is very difficult to actually put into practice. Even an old man of eighty cannot do it.

This answer is a very good description of the real situation in our life. The fact that something a three year old child can say, cannot be put into practice even by an eighty year old man shows us clearly the enormous gulf between what we think and say in words, and what we can actually do; theory and action exist in completely different worlds. We do not normally realize this simple fact in our daily lives. At school we are taught to use the viewpoint of a civilization which is based on a way of thinking that has been passed down the ages from the Greek idealists. This viewpoint is based on a belief that it is possible to understand all things and to solve all problems intellectually. Many people today react very strongly to the assertion that problems cannot be solved by thinking about them, but only by acting.

One significant fact which allows us to say that human beings are the most excellent of living creatures is that the human brain has been found to be heavier than the brain of an ape. We have more brain cells than our animal cousins. This capacity for thought is what distinguishes us from other animals. This fact has allowed the human race to position itself next to the gods in order of intellectual ability. This is the position in which western civilization places man in the chain of development. From this perspective, it is quite natural to conclude that we have the power to understand everything. Science is a child of man's great intellect, and the many developments in the fields of science have given us unparalleled benefits. Material progress has been so astonishing that we naturally feel that there is nothing that will not be understood given time. This natural feeling has become a well-rooted belief—that the intellect is supreme.

If we look at our daily life, however, we can see that we are deluding ourselves in this. Life doesn't work like that. We can go to a bookstore and be confronted with hundreds and hundreds of books on every subject under the sun. If we buy one and take it home and read it, it soon becomes clear that it cannot give us the fundamental answers to life's problems. Although we can accumulate a lot of information and knowledge, we are by and large unable to put this knowledge into practice in our real lives.

Gautama Buddha was confronted by the same kinds of problems. No matter how much we think about something, no matter how much knowledge we accumulate on a particular subject, even though we may make strenuous efforts to solve our particular problem, we find that it is in fact too difficult—we cannot actually do it. On the other hand, our efforts often lead us into doing things that we wanted to avoid doing. Sometimes it seems that we end up just repeating those very things that we were trying to avoid. So looking at our actual conduct in daily life, it is clear that we are actually very weak. Although our heads may be filled with great ideas, when we try to put them into practice, the result in the real world is always different from what we wanted. When we habitually live with the perfection of the ideas in our heads, and try to live our lives based on them, we will always be disappointed with the results of our efforts. This is the real situation.

Some people form an idea, and the idea itself causes them great suffering, because no matter how much effort they make, they can never put their idea into practice. Other people think that a wiser way to get along in life is just to throw away all ideas and aims and drift along following the situation. When people make serious efforts to reach their ideals they are bound to end up in failure, feeling miserable. And people who throw away all ideas and worries often find it difficult to maintain a reason for living. Living day by day just letting time roll on does not give us an aim in life. Although we can get some kind of satisfaction from sensual pleasures like eating, or spending money on fine clothes which make us feel good, there is a limit. Even if we become rich and live in grand houses it is still doubtful whether we really feel satisfied with our lives. This sort of situation is a common problem in life.

Gautama Buddha faced the same problem. At the time when he lived, the religion of Brahmanism had been dominant for several hundreds of years. Brahmanism teaches that the ultimate divine reality of the Universe is Brahma, from which all beings originate, and to which they all return. Thus the world in which we live is the image of Brahma. Human body, mind and spirit are all in the image of Brahma. These teachings encourage people to develop the elements of Brahma in themselves and so to become one with Brahma again, the ultimate state of human happiness. Brahmanism is believed to have emerged as a religion around 1200 or 1300 BC. Gautama Buddha lived in the 4th and 5th centuries BC, and so when he was born these teachings had already been established for a long time. Because of this, the teachings had degenerated and been corrupted, weakening the power of the religion when Gautama Buddha was alive.

At this time there was also a very powerful and active school of philosophy based on the teachings of six heretic teachers. Of the six, four were materialists who insisted that the world was based on matter and that ideals had no value. They rejected morality and pronounced that the aim of life was to satisfy the physical body. They denied the difference between good and bad. The other two taught a kind of skepticism in which they denied the existence of any kind of criteria for governing human societies. The school thus consisted of materialists and skeptics. In this situation, there was a confrontation between traditional Brahmanism and the teachings of the six philosophers.

We can imagine that from an early age Gautama Buddha must have anguished in deciding which of these systems he believed. Because of his sincere character, he must have tried hard to believe in Brahmanism, and must have been quite knowledgeable about that religion. But he was very sensitive to the question of whether Brahmanism was really believable, whether it was true or not. However, although he could not in the end believe in Brahmanism, he also found that the materialistic and skeptical teachings of the six philosophers could not satisfy him. In his struggle to find which system was true, he tried asceticism and he tried Zazen. After some time, early one morning on seeing the morning star, he realized that this world, here and now, is splendid. This is written in the Sutras: *"The earth and all living beings are splendid."*

This total acceptance of all things as they are gave Gautama Buddha a basis on which to form his thought. If we look at the many Buddhist Sutras written on the Buddha's realization we can conclude that he reached this viewpoint or state because he revered action. Action cannot exist at any other time or place than the present moment here and now. Another way of looking at this is in terms of past, present and future: no matter what mistakes we have made in the past, although we may regret them, we can never return to that past moment to put things right. It is clear that we cannot return to the past. At the same time, although we want to attain our dream or reach our aim in the future, we can never go into the future to reach our dream. But if we look at life as centered on acting, we see that we can only really exist in the present. We can never return to the past, and we cannot go into the future.

This is the essence of what Gautama Buddha taught—real existence is the present moment. Gautama Buddha reached the point where he saw clearly that living in the present moment just doing the best we can is the only realistic way to live. As long as we live in this way, there is nothing that we need fear, and no need to worry. The Universe moves forward under the rule of cause and effect. All that we have to do in our life is to live fully in the present. This is Gautama Buddha's teaching. And if we have this viewpoint, we can find nothing insurmountable in our life. Although problems will come and go, with sincere action, things will improve with the unfolding of causality. But we need to make efforts even in happy times to maintain this happy state. This is the real situation, and this is what Gautama Buddha taught. Centered on action, people can solve all their problems.

We are very fortunate that Gautama Buddha's teachings have come down the centuries to us, and we can feel his great benevolence. I urge people to study and follow these teachings with all their energy and live following the criteria of the Buddha's teachings on action.

CHAPTER NINE
ACTION AND DAILY LIFE
_____ ❧ _____

THE MAIN ACTIVITIES IN OUR day-to-day lives are centered around eating, sleeping and working, and include getting up, getting dressed, and so on. In my first talk I quoted Master Tendo Nyojo saying, *"The golden and splendid form is to get dressed and to eat meals."* This says that the real meaning of Gautama Buddha's splendor is in our daily activities of eating and dressing, just as it was for Gautama Buddha himself.

This is rather a unique assertion for a religion. Religions usually tell us that activities like eating and getting dressed are second in importance to spiritual faith. We generally think that a religion must value the spiritual side of life at the expense of daily activities like these. These daily activities don't seem grand enough to be the center of belief in a religion. This is the common perception.

But Buddhist philosophy is based around action, and so the activities of eating, getting dressed, washing ourselves—washing the face after getting up in the morning—these daily activities form the essence of Gautama Buddha's teachings.

In the Shobogenzo, there is a chapter called *Hatsu-U*, or the Buddhist Bowls. These bowls are called *patra* in Sanskrit, and *o-ryoki* in modern Japanese. In this chapter Master Dogen explains that eating meals is an important Buddhist practice. He says *"The patra is the body-and-mind of Buddhist patriarchs."* In this way, Master Dogen values the bowls very highly as a symbol of his religion.

Master Dogen also wrote a book called *Fushuku Han Ho* or Rules for Eating Meals. Traditionally, priests in temples in Japan eat rice gruel in the morning and rice at midday. The book sets down the rules of conduct when eating breakfast and lunch. He sets out the details of how meals should be eaten. When he was 23 years old, Master Dogen set off for China and stayed there living in temples for 4 years. During this time, he realized that the way of taking meals that the Chinese priests followed was a tradition, and he wanted to bring this traditional way of eating back to Japan and establish it here. He wanted people in Japan to follow the traditional way of eating exactly. One of the rules states that before starting to eat we should recite *Gokan No Ge* or the Five Reflections out loud. The Five Reflections are:

> *We reflect upon the insufficiency of our effort in this life.*
> *We contemplate the effort which has gone into the preparation of this meal.*

After the cold winter, people are planting rice seedlings and tending them through the summer. Then in the autumn the rice is harvested and threshed to give us grain to eat. If we think about the effort that goes into this, the work involved in pulling out weeds, supplying water to the rice fields when needed, and planting out the rice seedlings at the right time, just producing rice to eat involves lots of work. Not only rice, but also vegetables, and all other foods involve care and labor. We should reflect on how the food comes to our table. This is the first reflection.

We reflect upon our merit.
We know that we are not deserving of this meal.

We are allowed to become monks through the benevolence of many people, and we are thus given the chance to practice Buddhism. If we look at our Buddhist practice, we can never feel that we have done well enough. So we eat reflecting on the insufficiency of our conduct.

We reflect upon the sources of our mental illusions and mistakes.
We must avoid greed, anger, and ignorance.

We try not to be greedy, not to become angry, and not to complain. These are known as the three poisons. In Buddhism, avoiding these three states is part of our training in how to avoid unnecessary thoughts, doing wrong acts, making mistakes. We should avoid these states when we are eating meals.

We reflect upon the reason for eating meals. It is to avoid becoming weak and thin.

Buddhism says that food is a kind of effective medicine to stop us becoming weak, and meals are traditionally called "Great Medicine." This expression gives us an indication of the importance Buddhism places on eating meals. Although modern medical knowledge is highly developed and techniques are very advanced, meals are of prime importance in keeping us healthy, and medicines can only be of secondary importance. The food which we eat every day nourishes our body and keeps us from weakening. So from the Buddhist viewpoint, food really is good medicine, and we eat meals to stop us getting weak and thin. If we become weak we will lose the ability to work.

We reflect upon the ultimate reason for taking meals. It is only to attain the truth.

When we eat this meal now, we are grasping the truth of Buddhism. We eat not solely to nourish our body, but also as a practice to complete our task of attaining the Buddhist truth.

These are the five reflections.

On these matters, Master Kodo Sawaki, under whom I studied for many years, often said when he was teaching us: "Are we eating in order to work or working in order to eat! Although some people think that eating is the more important, and they work in order that they can eat with work as a secondary aim, in Buddhism the value of a human being comes from the work they do. It is not so important what we eat, it is simply that we have to eat in order to be able to work." This is what Sawaki Roshi often said. And this meaning is included in the five reflections.

Buddhism also reveres the value of the kasaya, the Buddhist robe.

In addition to its traditional view of meals, Buddhism also has a tradition in what we wear. There are two chapters in the Shobogenzo written about the kasaya: *Kesa Kudoku*, The Merit of the Kasaya, and *Den-e*, The Transmission of the Robe. *Kesa Kudoku* explains what the value of the kasaya is, and *Den-e* describes the kind of kasaya that priests wear, and refers to the robe as the heart and body of the Buddha.

The religion called Buddhism has been practiced for many years in India, Tibet, China, Japan and many countries of South-east Asia. Buddhists in all of these countries wear the kasaya, although the styles are somewhat different from country to country. Wearing the kasaya identifies us as Buddhists.

But the kasaya is not only a uniform which shows that we

are Buddhists. Wearing it also embodies the religion itself. People tend to think that clothes show the person, and nowadays there are many different fashions, materials, colors, and designs which allow us to express ourselves. Clothes express the history of humanity and tell us something about the wearer.

In the chapter in Shobogenzo titled *Senmen*, or Washing the Face, Master Dogen says that washing is very important. He quotes from the Lotus Sutra to make his point:

> *"The bodhisattva applies oil to the body,*
> *Having bathed away dust and dirt,*
> *And puts on a fresh and clean robe:*
> *Totally clean within and without."*

Master Dogen comments: *"So to bathe body-and-mind, to apply fragrant oil, and to get rid of dust and dirt, are Buddha-Dharma of primary importance."* He goes on to talk about washing the face: *"Washing the face has been transmitted from India in the west, and it has spread through China in the east."*

We tend to think that washing the face in our daily life is a small matter of no importance. But in fact, washing the face is a very important expression of our civilization. Looking back into Japanese history, in ancient times there was no custom of washing in hot water. They had the custom of *"misogi"* which was to wash in cold water. Then around the Nara Era, the practice of using hot water came to Japan with Buddhism, and started to become customary. The wife of Emperor Shomu is said to have built the first public bath, and this is the way that washing the body spread from being part of a religious custom into normal society. Washing our body to keep it clean and washing the face are both close indicators of the level of a civilization.

In this same chapter, Master Dogen also explains how to clean the teeth. He describes how to use a willow twig, a custom which came originally from India. Buddhist priests used to carry a twig of willow especially for this purpose when they traveled. Priests have to carry 18 special items with them when they travel, and the willow twig is the most important of these items.

So in Buddhism we find washing the face and cleaning the teeth set out as essential conduct for priests. Both customs came to Japan from India via China. Master Dogen laments the fact that, in his time, the practice of cleaning the teeth had virtually died out in China. He re-established the practice in his temple, Eihei-ji, and the priests there continue the same custom until this day. Master Dogen felt very thankful that he was able to re-establish these customs. He adds *"Before we have washed the face, to perform any of the various practices is impolite."* This clearly confirms that washing the face in the morning is a vital part of Buddhist conduct.

In another chapter titled *Senjo*, or Washing, we can find the passage: *"Water is not always originally pure or originally impure. The body is not always originally pure or originally impure."* This means that it is not whether the body is clean or dirty or whether the water is clean or dirty that is important. The meaning of washing in Buddhism is not only to wash our dirty body in clean water; Gautama Buddha taught us that the action of washing itself is important, and we follow his teachings. These teachings say that washing the body has an important religious meaning.

In the same chapter, Master Dogen instructs us to cut our fingernails. We do not normally think of cutting the fingernails as part of religious practice, but in Buddhism it forms an essential part of religious conduct. The chapter also contains detailed instructions on how to go to the toilet; what kind of preparation, and the way we should use the toilet. These things are written down in great detail.

We are especially told how important it is to keep the important private parts of the body clean. In modern Japan there is no custom to wash the bottom after going to the toilet, but that custom still exists in India. In hotels in India there is always a small hand bowl kept in the toilet for that purpose. You fill the bowl with water and use it to wash the bottom. These customs were transmitted to temples in China and when Master Dogen stayed there, he saw the customs and brought them back to Japan. This is what happened. We may suppose that he established the same customs in Eihei-ji temple too. These days most western countries use toilet paper. There are many different countries and customs. From among all these differing customs, as modern global society adopts the better of these one by one, civilization moves forward.

Looking around the world, we can see many and varied customs, some good, some not so good. In looking at different countries, I use one simple criterion in judging the level of that society—the state of the public toilets in that country. If the public toilets are clean, it shows that the level of civilization in that country is high. We should really make it a priority to keep public toilets clean, and in order to achieve this, people must first realize the importance of personal and public hygiene.

All these sorts of daily activities are clearly described in the Shobogenzo as religious conduct. Quoting Master Dogen again:

My late Master Tendo, the eternal Buddha ... says in his formal preaching in the lecture hall,

"I remember the following: A monk asks Hyakujo, 'What is something miraculous?' Hyakujo says 'Sitting alone on Great and Mighty Peak.' Monks, do not be disturbed. Let the fellow

kill himself by sitting for a while. If someone today were suddenly to ask, 'Acarya Nyojo, what is something miraculous?', I would only say to them 'What miracle could there be? Finally what is there to say? The patra of Joji has moved to Tendo and will eat meals.'"

So in reply to the question *'What is something miraculous?'*, Master Hyakujo says that sitting alone in his hut on the mountain is a most wonderful thing. Master Tendo tells us not to be surprised and to let Hyakujo go on practicing Zazen in his hut. He says that if someone were to come up to him and ask him right at this moment what the most wonderful thing is, he would reply that there are no such things as miracles in our everyday life. In the end he just tells everyone that on Mount Tendo, he is still using the bowls which he used in his old temple, Joji temple, everyday. He expresses this as a wonderful fact!

This kind of example is indeed the most wonderful thing. It shows that Buddhism is centered on action, and it also illustrates the accepting of the real situation in front of us in our day-to-day life—leading a sincere life. These are indeed Buddhist practices.

Nowadays, people usually have one of two basic attitudes to daily life: a positive, optimistic attitude, or a negative, critical attitude. I have the impression that the majority of people in modern societies have a critical, pessimistic or negative outlook: what should we do about nuclear weapons; what should we do to keep the earth free from pollution; how can we solve the ozone layer problem; how stupid humans are to create situations like Somalia; why are eastern European countries always fighting. These sorts of pessimistic worries are negative views and they are fairly widespread. But this is not the Buddhist way. We are living just at the moment of the present. We concentrate on and act in this moment. As long as we live by acting in the present moment, making our efforts to improve the situation, we are free from anguish and suffering.

Generally religions are thought to embrace this sort of "concerned" attitude but it is basically pessimistic. It comes from a belief that the world in which we live is full of sin and impurity. If we urge ourselves onward in making efforts to get rid of the evil face of the world so that only the good remains, we end up feeling anxious or pessimistic. This is the normal face of religion.

But Buddhism has no such outlook. There is no imperative to improve on reality. We accept the wonder of the world just as it is. The attitude of accepting things as they are is our natural or original state. If our behavior wanders away from the natural path, we generate our own dissatisfaction and start to complain. This is what leads us to a pessimistic and negative view of the world. Of course things happen in life to make us feel miserable sometimes, but the question is whether this kind of outlook is the right basic view.

This was the question that Gautama Buddha asked himself. After some years following the severe life of an ascetic, he finally found that this world is wonderfully positive as it is. And he wanted to tell everyone what he had found. He wanted to teach the fact to all people. This is the origin of the Buddhist religion. However many people doubt what I am saying. They believe that Buddhism is based on a pessimistic view, in which the world is full of suffering. They believe that Buddhism says that the world is suffering, and that our role is to accept this and to bear the suffering. They think that this is the Buddhist life. I strongly disagree.

The Shobogenzo contains no such belief. This is my understanding. On the contrary, Master Dogen tells us that we should accept the world in its splendor as it is. This is the fundamental principle in his teachings.

The reason why people think that Buddhism has such a pessimistic view of the world comes from the traditional interpretation of the Four Noble Truths. These four truths form the center of Buddhist belief. The traditional interpretation of these truths gives us a bleak picture of life, as if we should engage in a struggle in a world of suffering to banish all our desires and attain some special state. But this interpretation is not the only one. Here is another interpretation which I believe shows us clearly the Buddhist way in this world, and which is the interpretation consistent with Master Dogen's teachings.

The first Noble Truth is interpreted to mean that the world is full of suffering, but this truth is only one of four truths which must be taken together. It means that the world is full of suffering when we look at it in a certain way, with a certain viewpoint. If we look at the world from an idealistic point of view, compared to the perfection of the ideas in our heads, the world is far from perfect. It is this gap between our perfect ideas and the real world that causes us suffering.

The second Noble Truth says that if we leave the idealistic view, we can find an objective viewpoint: this world is just an accumulation of matter. This is a different, scientific view of the world. But solely from this view of the world we cannot find the ultimate value of life. That is, we tend to lose the aim of living.

In order to get rid of both these ways of looking at life, one which makes us suffer comparing our life with our ideals, and the other in which we cannot find the reason for living, we should enter the world of action. This is the third Noble Truth. The third truth urges us to deny the first two viewpoints. To stop complaining and feeling dissatisfied, to stop letting the situation carry us along; relying on our own actions we can start to make our own life. This is the meaning of the third

Noble Truth. If we live our lives centered around action we can live in oneness with the truth.

This oneness with the truth is the Path that we follow. This is the fourth Noble Truth. It urges us to follow the path of action in our day-to-day lives; to live our lives in oneness with the rule of the Universe.

If we look at the true meaning of the Four Noble Truths like this, they do not give a pessimistic view of the world; they teach us what we should do in order to be happy. This is the way that Buddhism teaches us to live our daily life.

CHAPTER TEN
BUDDHISM AND ZAZEN

CRSO

I HAVE EXPLAINED HOW THE TEACHINGS of Buddhism are centered in action. If we think about our actions in day-to-day life, we can see that, although thinking about our actions is easy, the problem of acting itself is difficult. We learn through experience how difficult it is to put an idea into practice.

The conversation between the Chinese poet Haku-Raku Ten and Master Choka Dorin illustrated this fact very clearly. Although a three year old child can say wise words, even an eighty year old man cannot put them into practice. Gautama Buddha realized how difficult it is to put an idea into practice. This is why one of his fundamental teachings is to urge us to live in the world of action.

If we reflect on our actual experience of acting in daily life, often we find that although we wanted to do something, to actually do it was very difficult. On the other hand, we often end up doing those very things that we try not to do, seemingly against our will. To overcome this problem is the fundamental task in our life.

If we look at life from the point of view of what we should or ought to do, if we are unable to do what we should do, we feel that we are not living with dignity. And if we cannot live how we want to live, we feel that we are less than human.

The ability to control ourselves is an extremely valuable thing in daily life. But nobody can deny that to be able to control ourselves as we would wish is extremely difficult. Gautama Buddha himself must have experienced this very human problem. In modern times, there are people who say that it is arrogant to believe that human beings can control themselves in this way, and that therefore we have no choice but to let matters take their own course and to go with the flow. This idea about life is especially widespread in Japan since the end of the second world war.

But Gautama Buddha denied the idea that the only way human beings can live is to follow things that happen in any particular circumstances. He used the word "buddha" to mean someone who is able to control themselves. He asserted clearly that human beings have the power to control themselves. Getting hold of themselves, they should make their efforts to follow right teachings and lead meaningful and happy lives.

People whose beliefs are founded on scientific materialism often have a common idea that, as we human beings are too weak to control ourselves, we should just follow what happens in the world, and float along with the stream. They feel that it is their duty to bear whatever situation they find themselves in. But Buddhism has no such teaching. Buddhism states that anyone can become a buddha as long as they have right thoughts and right ability, and self-control. In this state they can control their lives with complete freedom.

But how can we learn to control ourselves? Gautama Buddha gave us the practice of Zazen as a means to experience self-control. Zazen did not originate with Gautama Buddha; the history of Zazen goes back to its origins in yoga exercises. Some of these postures were similar to the present Zazen posture, and Gautama Buddha recognized the posture as the most correct posture which human beings could use as a standard. He said that when we practice Zazen we are buddha.

There is a chapter in the Shobogenzo called *Zanmai-O Zanmai*, The Samadhi which is King of Samadhis. Samadhi refers to the state in Zazen, the calm and serene state of body and mind. In this chapter Master Dogen asserts that the state in Zazen is the supreme state of calmness and serenity. The first paragraph says,

> "To transcend the whole Universe at once; to live a great and valuable life in the house of the Buddhist patriarchs is to sit in the full lotus posture. To tread over the heads of non-Buddhists and demons; to become, in the inner sanctum of the Buddhist patriarchs, a person in the concrete state, is to sit in the full lotus posture. To transcend the supremacy of the Buddhist patriarchs' supremacy there is only this one method."

Buddhist practice is not thinking about problems with the brain, or reacting to stimuli from the external world, it is just to act. You come back to your original self by sitting quietly with crossed legs and straight spine. This is Zazen. This is action. You are sitting as a person in reality, practicing and transcending the teachings of Gautama Buddha and the Universe. This is Zazen.

Master Dogen sometimes talked about Zazen as *shoshin tanza*, which means to correct our body and sit right. Zazen is the state in which we sit with right posture, not consciously trying to think anything, not consciously focusing on external stimuli.

In the chapter called *Bendowa*, A Talk about Pursuing the Truth, Master Dogen describes Zazen as *jijuyo zanmai*. He says that the standard state in Zazen is one of *jijuyo zanmai*, or receiving and using the self. This is a traditional phrase of describing the standard state. Let me talk in more detail about what the state of *jijuyo zanmai* refers to.

The basic Buddhist viewpoint is that the world neither consists of mind/spirit, nor of matter/things. The world is a synthesis of these two. Mind and matter are synthesized in reality in an indivisible oneness. They have never been separate.

Human beings are not just minds/spirits, nor are they just physical bodies; mind and body are indivisibly one originally and have never been divided. Thus in Buddhism, at the end of the day, it is impossible to say what a person is. Because in order to describe we must divide. This is Buddhism's fundamental assertion.

A characteristic of Buddhist philosophy is that every single theory within it has a physical fact with which to back it up. There are no theories in Buddhism for which we cannot find a supporting situation in the material world. In this situation, Master Dogen's description of the Buddhist state, *jijuyo zanmai* or the state of receiving and using the self, must have a counterpart in terms of the workings of the physical body.

Fortunately modern physiology has developed to the extent that we can now understand more clearly the workings of our bodies and the relationship with the Buddhist state of *jijuyo zanmai*. This was something the ancient Buddhist masters were unable to do. Their assertions were intuitive assertions.

Modern physiology has discovered that the involuntary workings of our bodies are controlled by the autonomic nervous system, which is, as its name implies, beyond our conscious control. Our internal organs, heart, liver, kidney, and so on are all controlled by this system of nerves in a way which we cannot consciously affect. For example, when we are excited our heart rate speeds up and it is impossible to make our heart beat more slowly by a simple act of will. We cannot stop our heart from beating, and in normal circumstances it goes on and on beating without our efforts until we die. The rhythm of the heart, now fast, now slow, is controlled automatically by our nervous system.

Physiologists have found that there are in fact two opposing systems within the autonomic nervous system. One system of nerves is called the sympathetic nerves, and they are responsible for our "fight or flight" reactions—for stimulating our metabolism and making us more aggressive. They make the heart beat faster. The other system is called the parasympathetic nervous system, and these nerves calm us down and make us more passive. They make the heart beat more slowly. All internal organs are controlled by both groups of nerves and can thus be stimulated or calmed, or something in between.

What Buddhism says is that our standard or original state is the state in which these two systems of nerves, the sympathetic nerves and the parasympathetic nerves, are balanced. In this state we are neither too aggressive, nor too passive.

Again, in Shobogenzo *Bendowa*, A Talk about Pursuing the Truth, Master Dogen says: "*the samadhi of receiving and using the self is its standard.*" The state in which the functioning of the sympathetic nerves and the parasympathetic nerves are balanced, something that we cannot consciously control, is the balanced state, the same as the state in Zazen. This is the standard of Zazen and the standard of the Buddhist path. However, it is impossible for us to reach this balanced state just by our will, because we are unable to control the balance of our autonomic nervous system. Gautama Buddha, through his own experience, found the fact that when we sit in the Zazen posture, the actions of our parasympathetic and sympathetic nervous systems become balanced. This is the standard or original state of human beings. Gautama Buddha urged us to adopt this method of Zazen as a practice that enables us to get back to our standard original state.

On this point, Zazen is a practice—something we need to do. We cannot balance our autonomic nervous system just by thinking, no matter how excellent our intellect is. But immediately we start to practice Zazen, the balanced state appears instantly. In the same chapter in Shobogenzo, it says: *"If a human being, even for a single moment, manifests the Buddha's posture in the three forms of conduct, while that person sits up straight in samadhi, the entire world of Dharma assumes the Buddha's posture and the whole of space becomes the state of realization."* This sentence means that when we practice Zazen, we can become buddha immediately; the state in Zazen is *being Buddha*. This is why Master Dogen says *"...even for a single moment..."* He wants to emphasize that Zazen itself is *instantaneously and immediately the state of buddha*. Some people believe that practicing Zazen is a way to become enlightened, but Master Dogen asserts that while practicing Zazen we are in the state of Buddha, the state of a balanced autonomic nervous system. All that we have to do to attain buddhahood is to practice Zazen. The idea that if we continue to practice Zazen, we can sometime in the future become a buddha is not Buddhism.

There is a story which illustrates this point. Master Baso Do-itsu, who was a disciple of Master Nangaku Ejo lived alone in a small hut. His master visited him one day and asked him *"What are you doing these days?"* Master Baso replied *"These days I just practice Zazen."* Then Master Nangaku asks him *"What is your aim in sitting in Zazen?"* Master Baso replied *"The aim of sitting in Zazen is to become buddha."* Master Nangaku promptly picks up a tile and polishes it on a rock near Baso. On seeing this, Baso asks *"What are you doing, Master?"* Nangaku says *"I am polishing a tile."* Baso says *"What is the use of polishing a tile?"* Nangaku says *"I am polishing it into a mirror."* Baso says *"How can polishing a tile make it into a mirror?"* Master Nangaku replies *"How can sitting in Zazen make you into a buddha?"*

Master Nangaku's final reply is his assertion that we cannot make ourselves into a buddha by practicing Zazen, since the state in Zazen *is* the state of buddha already. He wanted to show this to Master Baso clearly and unforgettably with his demonstration of doing the impossible by polishing a tile to make it a mirror.

At present I run a Zazen Dojo or Practice Center on the outskirts of Tokyo. When I look at the general situation in society here, I feel that Zazen practice in Japan has greatly deteriorated. I feel that if we are not able to revive the practice of Zazen, to make it flourish again, Buddhism will never prosper. I think that to set up many Zazen Dojos like ours throughout the country and throughout the world is the best way. To do that, to ensure that Zazen will flourish, we need the sponsorship of many companies and organizations. Unfortunately the situation here has still a long way to go. My great hope is that slowly, step by step, Zazen Dojos can be established, and that they will spread the practice of Zazen through the world, and Buddhism will flourish. The company which employs me organizes *sesshins* or Zazen retreats in a temple named Tokei-in in Shizuoka prefecture in May, June, August, September, and October. At each retreat, 40 or 50 of the company's employees spend two nights and three days in the temple practicing Zazen. If Zazen retreats like these, organized by companies, became popular, then the personnel managers in those companies would notice the benefits.

Let me tell you about my company's experience with the retreats we hold. For the duration of each retreat, participants have to follow the Buddhist traditional way of taking meals. When, for instance, one of the senior managers has his turn as a meal server, he has to bow to his newest and most junior members of staff and fill their bowls with rice or soup. The recipient bows down with hands joined in return. When I watch these customary ways of doing things being acted out between managers and junior staff members at mealtimes, I feel that it has great personal dignity for both sides.

Without having to give lectures to new junior staff members about how they should behave to their bosses, or to give management seminars to explain to managers how to treat their younger staff members as individuals and with respect, participating in a religious retreat together for a few days in shared circumstances teaches both sides naturally and practically how people in different positions in the company should behave towards each other. This is a direct teaching resulting from action in day-to-day life. This inevitably establishes a relationship between them based on mutual respect and dignity. It is far better than having to instruct people not to do this or to do that.

While on the subject of Zazen practice I would like to say something about the use of the *kyosaku*, the wooden stick used by some people to strike participants on the shoulders during Zazen practice to stop them dozing off. I once watched a documentary on the TV about new company employees straight out of school who were sent to a Zazen retreat as part of their induction course. During the retreat, a person there was using the *kyosaku* while the participants practiced. Later in the program, one of the participants was telling of his experiences on the retreat, and he said that he never wants to join a retreat again because of the indignity of receiving the *kyosaku*. I think that teaching people Zazen in this way is utterly wrong. Although the *kyosaku* is much used in Zazen practice today, I never use it. My reason is that Master Dogen never once mentioned the use of the *kyosaku* in any of his writings. He was meticulous in his descriptions of all the Buddhist customs and traditions. If he had approved of its use, he would have written about it, describing in detail its form and the way it is used. There is no such description in any of his works. This convinces me that the *kyosaku* was not used at all in his time. It is likely that people started to use it at a much later date.

Another reason against using the *kyosaku* is that it disturbs our practice. It is essential that we individually take responsibility for our own posture during Zazen as far as possible. Practice in which an authority figure makes us do it has little value. We must make ourselves practice. It is up to us to make sure that we are sitting straight. To use the *kyosaku* to wake practitioners up so that they will not embarrass themselves before the others is not useful.

The Zazen Dojo that I run is fairly small; about 12 or 13 people live there. One of my basic principles is that everyone there has their own private room. If people do not have their own private area, they cannot live as dignified individuals. When people come to practice over a period of several days they are able to stay together in a large guest room, where they can get to know each other. But for the people who live there permanently, privacy is essential. At the present time, the members of the Dojo include 2 Americans, one of whom is a priest, 2 Canadians, 1 British priest, 1 Australian, 1 German, 1 Israeli, and 4 Japanese, 2 of whom are nuns who belong to the Soto sect.

One thing that I have observed in common among my overseas students is that they are no longer able believe in and follow the teachings of Christianity or Judaism. Although some still think of Christianity or Judaism as their religion, they have a strong urge to study some other religion. I think that this illustrates clearly the point I made in my first talk. It shows the current of history in the west moving away from the idealistic religious period, to the emergence of the materialistic scientific period, with belief in religion losing its power towards the end of the 19th century.

Young people in the west today are faced with a situation in which they are unable to commit themselves to belief in the teachings of any of the existing traditional religions, and at the same time they find scientific materialism to be unfulfilling. They are seeking for a solution to that problem. I have met more than a few young westerners who have come to Japan because they have been anguishing over that problem. This is the situation today.

We need to set up many Zazen dojos all over the country so that foreigners as well as Japanese people can study Buddhism and practice Zazen in day-to-day life. Some of those people would become monks and they would form the basis for leading the daily life based on Zazen. I hope also that ordinary people would then start to practice Zazen in their daily lives in society, so that slowly the number of people living this life would increase. I am looking forward to the time when many companies and organizations will want to provide facilities where people can come to enjoy the practice of Zazen.

In the last few years I have been studying a book entitled Mulamadhyamakakarika that is written in Sanskrit by a famous Indian Buddhist, Master Nagarjuna. I have confirmed in his writings in the Mulamadhyamakakarika exactly the same teachings based on action as in the writings of Master Dogen. Two great and revered thinkers, Master Nagarjuna and Master Dogen both base their teachings around the same center of action. In today's world, there are many interpretations of Buddhist thought, but I am convinced that, at the highest level, Buddhist theory is based on a philosophy of action.

The Cold War has ended, and the United States and the Soviet Union are on friendly terms. In the not too distant future, the world is going to become one politically and economically. With the emergence and implementation of the concept of political integration throughout the world, the realization that from all the ideas and philosophies which have emerged from the human mind, there is only one true viewpoint on reality, will also become clear. I believe firmly that the time has come. Instead of centering our way of thinking only around ideas, ideals, and spiritual aims, or only around the scientific and objective view of the material world in front of our eyes, human beings will start to look at reality centered on action. Our philosophical thought will reflect this, and gradually it will become embedded in our societies throughout the world. Then we can truly say that the world has become one.

Japan is one of the few countries in the world where true Buddhism still remains, particularly in the teachings of Master Dogen in the Shobogenzo. These teachings explain the philosophy of action. If people here can understand his teachings and learn to explain them to people in other parts of the world, it is possible for those teachings to spread through the world. If the philosophy of action spreads through the world, then the world can become stable and peaceful. If I think about the direction in which the world must move to attain peace, there is no other way.

I am sure that many people feel that what I am saying sounds too optimistic, that the world is a very complex place and the answer to world peace is not so easy. But the fact that the world is moving towards a single political system suggests very strongly that the way that people in different parts of the world view life is also slowly becoming unified. On this point, it is very important for people in Japan to try to understand the ultimate philosophical viewpoint of Buddhism and to teach it to other people in the world. It may be the most important historical task that we have here in Japan.

Buddhism, of course, is not only a philosophical system,

but is teachings based on the practice of Zazen. By practicing Zazen people can find the basis for the philosophical viewpoint of Buddhism. When someone has grasped what Zazen is through experience, and if they study and understand the ultimate philosophy of Buddhism, then they are able to explain to the world why practicing Zazen is so important to mankind. At every moment I reaffirm my hope that people will be able to follow this path. Of course it will take decades, or maybe even centuries to achieve. I do not think that it will happen in my own lifetime. But I have no room for doubt that the time is coming when the entire world shares a common viewpoint, and that from this fact, the entire world finds stability and peace. It is the natural result of the thousands of years that mankind has spent searching and building without ceasing.

Talking like this—some would say like a modern-day Don Quixote—living every day with this hope, I have come to believe that one day it will actually happen here in this real world in front of us—that it is mankind's common destiny.